Notre Dame De Paris

BELL'S HANDBOOKS TO
CONTINENTAL CHURCHES

NOTRE DAME DE PARIS

NOTRE DAME AND THE PONT DE L'ARCHEVÊQUE.

(From an etching by C. Méryon.)

NOTRE DAME DE PARIS

A SHORT HISTORY & DESCRIPTION OF THE CATHEDRAL, WITH SOME ACCOUNT OF THE CHURCHES WHICH PRECEDED IT

BY

CHARLES HIATT

AUTHOR OF
" CHESTER CATHEDRAL," " BEVERLEY MINSTER "
" WESTMINSTER ABBEY," ETC., ETC.

WITH FORTY-ONE ILLUSTRATIONS

LONDON : GEORGE BELL & SONS 1902

PREFACE

THE task of writing an account of the cathedral of Notre
Dame is materially lightened by the minute details of its
history and architecture to be found in the various writings
of M. Viollet-le-Duc, of which, unfortunately, the Library
of the British Museum does not contain a complete set.
The *Description de Notre Dame*, published in 1856 by
M. de Guilhermy in conjunction with M. Viollet-le-Duc,
contains much useful material, while the splendidly illustrated
account of the church in the first volume of *Paris à travers
les Ages* is full of interesting archæological particulars   As
the numerous other authorities which have been used are
quoted in the text, it is unnecessary to enumerate them here.
The writer has found Mr. Charles Herbert Moore's *Development of Gothic Architecture* useful in not a few difficult
matters.   He wishes specially to thank Mr. Edward Bell for
valuable suggestions on many important points.

CHARLES HIATT.

CHELSEA,
    October, 1902.

CONTENTS

LIST OF ILLUSTRATIONS

NOTRE DAME FROM THE SOUTH.

NOTRE DAME FROM THE QUAI ST. BERNARD.

NOTRE DAME DE PARIS.

CHAPTER I.

A BRIEF HISTORICAL ACCOUNT OF THE CATHEDRAL.

No city of the modern world has seen such amazing changes as the French metropolis. In the eyes of many persons, from every downfall Paris has arisen more incontestably splendid. But not to all is the Paris of Baron Hausmann lovelier than the city which preceded it. For instance, M. Joris-Karl Huysmans, the author at once modern and mystical of *A Rebours* and *La Cathédrale,* bitterly regrets the disappearance of those ancient and brooding byways which lent to the Paris of his youth a curious charm which has now almost disappeared. The Paris of magnificent vistas is at least less fascinating to the artist than the comparatively provincial city of crooked lanes which has gone to make way for a series of lofty and pretentious street fronts and spacious squares.

3

Strange it is that, where so much has been changed, the cathedral church of Notre Dame has remained almost unaltered in outline and general effect.   Revolutions have surged round it ; monstrous rites have been perpetrated within it ; even the hail of shot and shell have left this wonderful Gothic creation poorer only in decorative detail.   There is a certain fascination in the grimness of this mysterious building in *la ville lumière*, and I am disposed to agree with Mr. Richard Whiteing that it symbolises the underlying sadness, as opposed to the super-ficial gaiety of the Parisian.   Thousands of French churches are dedicated to Notre Dame : even in Paris itself we have Notre Dame de l'Assomption, Notre Dame de l'Abbaye aux Bois, Notre Dame des Blancs-Manteaux, Notre Dame des Champs, Notre Dame de Lorette, and Notre Dame des Victoires.   But still when we speak of Notre Dame we allude instinctively to that vast edifice which frowns over the slow and winding Seine.   The cathedral church of Notre Dame is almost as closely connected with the history of the French people as is the Abbey of Westminster with that of the English.   And indeed the gray-white building whose founda-tions are nearly washed by the waters of the Seine has seen pageants more superb, and tragedies more luridly dramatic, that our own proud Minster of the West.   Although it can boast no such marvellous continuity of vital historic episodes, Notre Dame is the one building in the French metropolis which seems to stand as a symbol for the whole city in all its memorable phases : with it may not be compared the bragging grandeur of the Arc de Triomphe, the extensive splendour of the Louvre, nor the rebuilt Hôtel de Ville. We do not forget the exquisite beauties of La Sainte Chapelle, the strange fascination of the resting-place of the Great Napoleon, nor the majesty of the once royal church of Saint Denis.   None of these, however, will bear serious comparison with the great Metropolitan Cathedral of Paris.   Notre Dame has an almost unearthly power of asserting its existence. Neither in full sunshine, nor in the twilight, nor when night has finally set in, will it allow its majestic proportions to be overlooked.   Mr. Henley has finely spoken of "the high majesty of Paul's," but even our own metropolitan cathedral, with its overwhelming dome, is scarcely more predominant than Notre Dame.

The geographical position of the Cathedral of Paris is not unlike that anciently possessed by Westminster Abbey, and by that crown of the Fens, Ely Cathedral. We find that Notre Dame dominates an islet of the Seine. At its east end is that tragical commentary on the life of modern Paris, The Morgue. The late Mr. Grant Allen, with a cheerfulness which we are far from sharing, noted that this triumphant example of the best Gothic in the world has often been restored. We believe that he was one of many intelligent persons who derive a real satisfaction from the so-called "restoration" of an ancient work, of which no real "restoration" is possible, though repair is an obvious duty.

The mediæval churches of western Europe nearly all claim a pre-Christian origin. It is charming to the mind of a certain type of antiquary to discover the origin of a Christian cathedral in the wreck of a Roman temple. For Westminster Abbey and for St. Paul's Roman foundations have, with more or less accuracy, been described. In the case of Notre Dame it is certain that the remains of an altar of Jupiter were discovered in 1711, which would seem to indicate that a pagan temple once stood on or near the site in the Gaulish city of Lutetia Parisiorum. In point of fact, it is a matter of no small difficulty to make out clearly the origin of Notre Dame, or to describe with certainty the ecclesiastical buildings which in the dim past occupied its site. A lady writer who has discussed the church with much intelligence writes on this matter as follows: [1]

"The origin of Notre Dame is enveloped in mystery. Whether its first bishop, St. Denis, or Dionysius, was the Areopagite converted by St. Paul's preaching at Athens, and sent by St. Clement to preach the Gospel to the Parisians, or whether he was another personage of the same name who was sent into Gaul in the third century and martyred during the persecutions under Decius, it is impossible to say, as there is no evidence of any value. Certain it is, however, that the first bishop of Paris bore the name of Denis, and that he suffered martyrdom, with his two companions Rusticus and Eleutherius, on the summit of the hill now called Montmartre. Tradition went so far as to point out the spot where they first gathered their followers together—the crypt of Notre Dame

[1] *The Churches of Paris*, by S. Sophia Beale: London, W. H. Allen and Co., 1893.

des Champs ; also the prison where our Lord appeared to them and strengthened them with His Holy Body and Blood at St. Denis de la Chartre ; the place, at St. Denis du Pas, where they suffered their first tortures ; and lastly, Montmartre, where they were beheaded. But, with the exception of the latter, all these holy spots have disappeared. So, too, have the crosses which marked the route taken by the Saint, when he carried his head to the place chosen for his burial, at St. Denis. An ancient church covered the remains of the three saints until the present splendid building was erected, in the reign of Dagobert I. Under the Roman dominion, Paris was comprised in the fourth Lyonnaise division, of which Sens was the metropolis. Hence the bishops of Paris acknowledged the Archbishop of Sens as their primate until 1622, when, at the request of Louis XIII., Pope Gregory XV. raised Paris to the see of an archbishopric. The succession has consisted of one hundred and nine bishops and fifteen archbishops, eight of whom have been raised to the dignity of Cardinal. Besides St. Denis six have been venerated as Saints : Marcel, in the fifth century ; Germain, in the sixth century ; Ceran, Landry, and Agilbert in the seventh, and Hugues in the eighth century."

We must leave this ancient and hazy story of saints and martyrs, and return to the thorny question of the origin of the cathedral. From the brief account of Notre Dame by Mr. A. J. C. Hare in his entertaining volume on Paris, we glean that about the year 375 a church, dedicated to St. Stephen (St. Etienne), was built on the islet under Prudentius, eighth bishop of Paris. "In 528," says Mr. Hare, "through the gratitude of Childebert—'*le nouveau Melchisedech*'—for his recovery from a sickness by St. Germain, another far more rich and beautiful edifice (dedicated to Sainte Marie—) arose by the side of the first church, and was destined to become *ecclesia parisiaca*, the cathedral of Paris. Childebert endowed it with three estates—at Chelles-en-Brie, at La Celle near Monterau, and at La Celle near Fréjus—which last supplied the oil for its sacred ordinances. The new church had not long been finished when La Cité, in which the monks of S. Germain had taken refuge with their treasures, was besieged by the Normans ; but it was successfully defended by Bishop Gozlin, who died during the siege. It is believed that the substructions of this church were found during recent excavations in the Parvis Notre Dame,[1] and architectural fragments then discovered are now preserved at the Palais des Thermes." It may be taken for granted that Childebert's church took the form of a Roman basilica, and it is probable that Roman materials were used in its construction. In 1847 further Roman remains were discovered on the site which doubtless formed part of Childebert's building. Some of them are preserved at the Hôtel-Cluny.

I am, however, inclined to agree with M. de Guilhermy and M. Viollet-le-Duc,[2] that the story of the cathedral previous to the episcopacy of Bishop Maurice de Sully (1160-96) is, if not absolutely fictitious, at least merely conjectural.

This prelate—generally counted as the sixty-second occupant of the see—seems at first to have united the adjacent churches of St. Stephen and Ste Marie on the Ile de la Cité, and then (without immediately and totally destroying them) to have commenced a new one on the same site, of which Pope Alexander III. laid the foundation-stone in 1163. Rapid progress must have been made with the work, for it is certain that in 1185 Heraclitus, patriarch of Jerusalem, officiated at the altar, in front of which, in the year following, Geoffrey, Count of Brittany, son of Henry II. of England, was buried. Maurice de Sully provided for the continuation of the work after his death, which took place in 1196. By his will he left five thousand *livres* in order that the choir might be roofed with lead. At this time, according to Viollet-le-Duc, considerable progress must have been made with the nave. Maurice de Sully was succeeded by Eudes de Sully (1197-1208), on whose death the see was occupied, until 1219, by Pierre de Nemours. Towards 1223 the west front was completed to the base of the great gallery, and by 1235 the towers were left much as we see them to-day. The spires, which it is generally admitted they were intended to carry, were never added.

[1] The space to the west of the church was called *Parvis paradisus*, the earthly paradise leading by the celestial Jerusalem.

[2] See *Description de Notre-Dame, Cathédral de Paris* : Paris, 1856. The main points of Viollet-le-Duc's inventory of the cathedral will be found in Queyron's *Histoire et Description de l'Eglise de Notre Dame*. Paris : E. Plon, Nourrit et Cie.

Between the years 1235 and 1240, a fire seems to have broken out at Notre Dame. On this subject history is silent, but that it did serious damage is maintained by Viollet-le-Duc on what appear to be sufficient grounds. According to him, repair was made in haste, so that rose windows, flying buttresses and other structural details were ruthlessly sacrificed. The west front seems to have escaped mutilation. Up to 1245 the cathedral, vast as was its area, possessed either no chapels at all, or chapels of inconsiderable dimensions. In that year, however, the addition of new chapels was proceeded with. It would appear that, shortly after, the plainness of the transept fronts in comparison with the splendidly decorated west façade was acutely felt. In 1257, Jean de Chelles was engaged on reconstructing the southern doorway. At this time St. Louis was King of France, and Renaud de Corbeil bishop of Paris. The northern door and the chapels next the transepts on either side were altered immediately after the southern entrance. In 1351, Jean Ravy and Jean de Bouteiller were engaged about the cathedral as sculptors.

During the next three centuries Notre Dame escaped anything in the nature of important change, destruction or addition; but in 1699 an era of reckless mutilation began. Between the last-named date and 1753 the Cloister, the stalls of the sixteenth century, the old high altar, many sepulchral monuments, and a vast quantity of stained glass were destroyed. The work done in the names of " repair " and " beautification " deprived the cathedral of mouldings, foliated capitals, gargoyles and pinnacles. The damage inflicted by the architect Soufflot (who designed the Panthéon) will be noticed later. Towards the end of Louis XV.'s reign the church was refloored with squares of marble. The new pavement involved the tearing up of a number of curious tombstones, some of which covered the dust of men greatly distinguished in French history. Between 1773 and 1787 minor alterations in the taste of the time were made in various parts of the building, but further additions were brought to an end by the outbreak of the Revolution. That any sculpture of a religious or royal character was spared at Notre Dame during that terrific upheaval seems to have been due to the eloquence of Citoyen Chaumette and the influence of Citoyen Dupuis. Of the great work of repair and addition performed by the architects

Viollet-le-Duc and Lassus, their assistants and successors, much will be said when we consider the cathedral in detail.

We have already discussed the early story of Notre Dame, and noted the vicissitudes through which the fabric has passed. I propose, before concluding this introductory chapter, to state in the briefest possible way the great historical events with which the cathedral is connected, from the death, in 1196, of Maurice de Sully to the present time.

From the tenth century up to the end of the fifteenth century the extraordinary *Fête des Fous* was celebrated in Notre Dame One of the cathedral employés was elected *Evêque des Fous*, and, wearing the actual vestments used in religious services, was honoured with a great banquet accompanied with grotesque dances and songs. This orgy took place in the church itself, and was so popular that it flourished in spite of the most determined efforts to suppress it. A similar custom was observed in La Sainte Chapelle. During the early years of the thirteenth century the Dominican order was established. St. Dominic himself preached once at least in Notre Dame. During his prayer before the sermon, the Virgin is said to have appeared to him in a cloud of light and to have given to him a book containing the subject-matter of his discourse. Raymond VII., Count of Toulouse, underwent the discipline of the lash for heresy before the door of the cathedral in 1229. This spot was for centuries occupied by a pillory. From 1220 onwards a series of disputes took place between the officials of the church and the university. During the long reign of St. Louis, which ended in 1271, the power of the bishop and chapter of Paris had increased enormously, and a host of vassals did homage to Bishop Etienne II. for their lands. The body of St. Louis was laid in state in Notre Dame previous to its burial at St. Denis. This custom was followed in the case of many other French monarchs and princes of the blood.

On April 10th, 1302, Philippe-le-Bel held the first meeting of the States-general in the cathedral. In the month of June, 1389, Isabeau de Bavière made a solemn entry into Paris. Froissart tells us that: "Devant ladite église de Notre-Dame, en la place, l'évêque de Paris étoit revêtu des armes de Notre-Seigneur et tout le collège. Aussi on moult avoit grand clergé et la descendit la royne et la mirent hors de sa litière les quatre ducs qui là estoyent, Berry, Bourgogne, Touraine et Bourbon. . . . La royne de France fut adestrée et menée parmy l'église et le chœur jusqu'au grand autel et la se mit A genoux et fit ses oraisons ainsi que bon lui sembla, et bailla et offrit à la trésorerie de Notre-Dame quatre draps d'or et la belle couronne que les anges lui avoient posée sur la porte de Paris."

A great thanksgiving service was held when Charles VI. had been saved from burning. The King, it may be recalled, was dressed as a satyr at a palace fête with five companions. The Duke of Orleans was curious as to the identity of the disguised, and approached them with a torch, which accidentally set their clothing alight. The King was saved by the Duchess de Berri, who threw a cloak over him, but four of his companions were burned to death.

We must now turn to the time of Henry V. of England, who, after Agincourt, became Regent of France with the right of succession to the throne. After his marriage with Catherine, daughter of Charles VI., in 1420, he paid a solemn state visit to Notre Dame. On Henry's death his son, afterwards Henry VI., was crowned King of France in the cathedral. When the English were driven from Rouen, a great service of thanksgiving was held to celebrate the entry of Charles VII. into the Norman capital.

"In the annals of Notre Dame," says Mr. W. F. Lonergan in his *Historic Churches of Paris*, "from the days of Louis XI, the rebellious dauphin who succeeded his father, Charles VII., to the reign of the fourteenth Louis, there is chiefly a long record of *Te Deums* after the victories of the French army. Historic Rheims, where Clovis had been baptized by S. Remi in 496, was the favoured city of the Merovingians, who had accorded it great privileges." Amongst these was the right of crowning and consecrating the Kings of France. Save Henri Quatre and Louis XVIII., all of them were crowned at Rheims ; but it was the custom of the newly made sovereigns to go in state to Notre Dame at Paris to return thanks for their advent to the throne. Amongst the most interesting of the historic events which took place in, or were magnificently celebrated at Notre Dame, were the following: the French victory over the Venetians at Agnadel

QUEEN MARIE ANTOINETTE RETURNING THANKS FOR THE BIRTH
OF A DAUPHIN, JANUARY 21ST, 1782.

(From " Paris à travers les Ages.")

or, as the Italians call it, Vaila, in 1509 ; the marriage of
Louis XII. with Mary, sister of Henry VIII. of England ;

the victories of Francis I. ; and the marriage of Mary Stuart with the Dauphin. The marriage of Henri, King of Navarre, with Marguerite de Valois, took place at the entrance to the cathedral, as the King was a Protestant. In 1590 the Catholic nobles swore at the altar of Notre Dame to fight this same Henri to the bitter end. In 1593, however, he became a Catholic, and attended mass at the cathedral on the occasion of his accession to the throne as the first monarch of the Bourbon line. The metropolitan see was raised to the dignity of an archbishopric by Pope Gregory XV. in 1622. In 1682, under Louis XIV., the great bell or *bourdon* of the church was christened Emmanuel Louis Thérèse, the King and Queen being the sponsors. Later on, in 1699, the great changes in the church, undertaken in fulfilment of the vow of Louis XIII., were begun. The first stone of the new altar was laid by the Archbishop with the utmost pomp. The foundation slab was inscribed : " Louis the Great—son of Louis the Just—after he had suppressed heresy, established the true faith in his kingdom, terminated gloriously wars by land and sea, wishing to accomplish the vow of his father, built this altar in the cathedral church of Paris, dedicating it to the God of Arms, Master of Peace and Victory, under the invocation of the Virgin, patron and protector of his State. A.D. 1699." During the reign of the "Grand Monarque," *Te Deums* were even more frequent than before.

We come at length to the part played by the cathedral during the Revolution. We need say nothing of the fate of the fabric itself, for that has already been alluded to. Its escape is little short of marvellous. The result of the sack of the treasuries of the churches of Paris is best told in Carlyle's vivid translation of Mercier : " This, accordingly, is what the streets of Paris saw : Most of these persons were still drunk, with the brandy they had swallowed out of chalices ;—eating mackerel on the patenas ! Mounted on Asses, which were housed with Priests' cloaks, they reined them with Priests' stoles ; they held clutched with the same hand communion-cup and sacred wafer. They stopped at the doors of Dram-shops ; held out ciboriums : and the landlord, stoup in hand, had to fill them thrice. Next came Mules high laden with crosses, chandeliers, censers, holy-water vessels, hyssops ;—

recalling to mind the Priests of Cybele, whose panniers, filled with the instruments of their worship, served at once as storehouse, sacristy and temple." On November 10th, 1793, the Cult of Reason was decreed by the Convention, and Notre Dame converted into the temple of the new religion. To quote Carlyle again: " For the same day, while this brave Carmagnole-dance has hardly jigged itself out, there arrive Procureur Chaumette and Municipals and Departmentals, and with them the strangest freightage : a New Religion ! Demoiselle Candeille, of the Opera ; a woman fair to look upon, when well rouged ; she borne on palanquin shoulder high ; with red woollen nightcap; in azure mantle ; garlanded with oak ; holding in her hand the Pike of the Jupiter-*Peuple*, sails in : heralded by white young women girt in tricolor. Let the world consider it ! This, O National Convention, wonder of the universe, is our New Divinity ; *Goddess of Reason*, worthy, and alone worthy of revering. Her henceforth we adore. Nay, were it too much of an august National Representation that it also went with us to the *ci-devant* Cathedral called of Notre Dame, and executed a few strophes in worship of her ? . . . . And now after due pause and flourishes of oratory, the Convention, gathering its limbs, does get under way in the required procession towards Notre Dame ;—Reason, again in her litter, sitting in the van of them, borne, as one judges, by men in the Roman costume ; escorted by wind-music, red nightcaps, and the madness of the world. And so, straightway, Reason taking seat on the high-altar of Notre Dame, the requisite worship or quasi-worship is, say the Newspapers, *executed*; National Convention chanting ' the *Hymn to Liberty*, words by Chénier, music by Gossee.' It is the first of the *Feasts of Reason* ; first communion-service of the New Religion of Chaumette." The real heroine of this orgy was probably an opera dancer called Maillard. ' Demoiselle Candeille ' was an actress and writer of some repute, who strenuously denied that she ever had anything to do with the Feast of Reason. An imitation " mountain " was erected in the nave for the " fête," on which was built a Gothic temple inscribed *A la Philosophie*. Around were busts of famous philosophers, and below an altar surmounted with the so-called Torch of Truth. The goddess sat on the hill, hymns were sung in her honour and vows of fidelity to her were taken. In 1794

the church was used as a bonded store for the wine seized in
the cellars of guillotined or outlawed Royalists. The month
of May in the same year saw the "Temple of Reason" turned
into that of the "Supreme Being," for Robespierre persuaded
the Convention to sign a decree recognising "the consoling
principle of the Immortality of the Soul." In 1795 Christian
worship was once more restored at Notre Dame. Nothing
of great importance happened to the church until the star
of Napoleon rose—until, indeed, the first Consul had become
Emperor.

Of all the magnificent ceremonies of which Notre Dame has
been the scene, the most splendid was the joint coronation of
Napoleon and Josephine in the winter of 1804. A full account
of it will be found in the *Mémoires de la Duchesse d'Abrantès*,
of which I quote a part, purposely leaving it in the original
French, as any translation would be comparatively colourless
and unpicturesque : "Le pape arriva le premier. Au moment
où il entra dans la basilique, le clergé entonna *Tu es Petrus*,
etc. ; et ce chant grave et religieux fit une profonde impression
sur les assistants. Pie VII. avançait du fond de cette
église, avec un air à la fois majestueux et humble. . . .
L'instant qui réunit peut-être le plus de regards sur les marches
de l'autel, fut celui où Joséphine reçut de l'empereur la
couronne et fut sacrée solennellement impératrice des Français.
Lorsqu'il fut temps pour elle de paraître activement dans le
grand drame, l'impératrice descendit du trône et s'avança vers
l'autel, où l'attendait l'empereur, suivie de ses dames du palais
et de tout son service d'honneur, et ayant son manteau porté
par la princesse Caroline, la princesse Julie, la princesse Elisa
et la princesse Louis. . . Je vis tout ce que je viens de dire dans
les yeux de Napoléon. Il jouissait en regardant l'impératrice
s'avancer vers lui ; et lorsqu'elle s'agenouilla . . . lorsque les
larmes qu'elle ne pouvait retenir, roulèrent sur ses mains
jointes qu'elle élevait bien plus vers lui que vers Dieu, dans ce
moment où Napoléon, ou plutôt *Bonaparte*, était pour elle
sa véritable providence, alors il y eut entre ces deux êtres une
de ces minutes fugitives, unique dans toute une vie, et qui
comblent le vide de bien des années. L'empereur mit
une grâce parfaite à la moinde des actions qu'il devait faire.
pour accomplir la cérémonie. Mais ce fut surtout lorsqu'il
s'agit de couronner l'impératrice. Cette action devait être

accompli par l'empereur, qui, apres avoir reçu la petite couronne fermée et surmontée de la croix, qu'il fallait placer sur la tête de Joséphine, devait la poser sur sa propre tête, puis la mettre sur celle de l'impératrice. Il mit à ces deux mouvements une lenteur gracieuse qui était remarquable.   Mais lorsqu'il en fut au moment de couronner enfin celle qui était pour lui, selon un préjugé, son *étoile heureuse* il fut *coquet* pour elle, si je puis dire le mot. Il arrangeait cette petite couronne qui surmontait la diadème, en diamant, la plaçait, la déplaçait, la remettait encore, il semblait qu'il voulût lui promettre que cette couronne lui serait douce et legère."

Napoleon, on this occasion, hastily took his crown from the Pope's hands and placed it haughtily on his own head— a proceeding which doubtless startled his Holiness.   In May 1814 Louis XVIII. and his family attended mass at Notre Dame after their entry into Paris.   A great service was held there in 1840, to celebrate the restoration of the remains of Napoleon I. to French soil, while Archbishops Affre, Sibour and Darboy, who died violent deaths, were commemorated with fitting solemnities.

The marriage of Napoleon III. to Eugénie de Montijo, Comtesse de Teba, on January 29th, 1853, was the occasion of a great display of gorgeous pageantry at Notre Dame, as was the baptism of the ill-fated Prince Imperial in 1857.   The Terrorists of 1871 robbed the treasury of the cathedral of many valuable relics, but their intention to injure the fabric itself was prevented by the timely arrival of troops.   The most notable ceremonies during the existence of the present Republic have been the funeral service, in June 1894, for President Carnot, assassinated in that year at Lyons, and the splendid State funeral of Louis Pasteur in October 1895.

The great festivals of the Church are celebrated at Notre Dame on a scale of almost unrivalled magnificence.   On Assumption Day, in particular, splendid music, wedded to the most ornate ritual, produces an effect never to be forgotten. The pulpit of the metropolitan cathedral has been occupied by a succession of great preachers, amongst them Bossuet and Bourdaloue, and the services and conferences are noted throughout the Roman Catholic world.   The Dominican Lacordaire began in 1835 a series of majestic and picturesque discourses, which earned for him the title *le Romantique de la*

Chaire, and he has been described as filling as a preacher the place occupied in literature by Victor Hugo and in painting by Delacroix, H. Vernet, and Delaroche. In recent times among the most popular pulpit orators have been the fiery Jesuit Père Ravignan, Monseigneur d'Hulst, Père Monsabré, and M. Hyacinthe Loyson, better known to fame as Père Hyacinthe.

Needless to say, this is the merest outline of the wonderful history of the Cathedral Church of Paris. If the columns of Notre Dame could speak, they would—to adapt a phrase of Viollet-le-Duc—be able to recount the history of France from the time of Philip Augustus to our own day. It is therefore natural that the whole French nation has for Notre Dame a feeling of veneration and affection similar to that which is called forth in English hearts by the Abbey Church of Westminster.

c

THE CHEVET.

CHAPTER II.

THE PLACE OF NOTRE DAME IN THE DEVELOPMENT OF FRENCH GOTHIC.

THE place of the Cathedral of Paris in the evolution of French Gothic [1] is so important that I propose to devote a brief chapter to it. The subject is essentially technical, but I will endeavour to make it as easy of comprehension as possible. The reader will doubtless ask himself what is the difference between Gothic and the style which preceded it. The reply, unfortunately, cannot consist of a dogmatic statement. The subject is a great one, and only a few sentences of this handbook may be devoted to it. I shall rely for the most part on the materials for a definition of Gothic given by M. Viollet-le-Duc in his *Dictionnaire Raisonné de l'Architecture Française*. The question is one of essential structural peculiarity as opposed to mere decorative idiosyncracy. I am aware that many English writers whose opinions are entitled to respect hold views in conflict with those here maintained. The style which immediately preceded Gothic is known generically as Romanesque. In Romanesque the system may be described as one of inert stability: in Gothic the system is one of scientifically calculated thrusts and counter-thrusts. It was the affair of art to inform what one may call the mechanics of the building with interest and beauty. There have been many attempts to compromise the two systems, so that we often find Romanesque features in obviously Gothic buildings. Much will be said in subsequent pages of the vaulting of Notre Dame. I would willingly have left this vexed question alone, but were I so to do, this handbook would be little more

[1] French Gothic is here generally intended to convey the Gothic of the Ile-de-France. The contemporary architecture of Normandy has a character of its own, probably not less valuable than that of the Ile-de-France. But it is different, and its differences have been dealt with in other handbooks of this series.

than a descriptive catalogue of objects of interest together with some historical reminiscences. For the vaulting is of the essence of the whole matter : compared with it the consideration of mouldings and of ornament is relatively unimportant. To put the matter plainly, the very existence of a Gothic church depends upon the proper arrangement of what we may call its mechanism—*i.e.* its vaulting, piers, buttresses and so forth. The mechanics being duly devised, art steps in, and renders the essential beautiful.[1]

It is not at Paris that we can trace the first attempt to break away from the principles of Romanesque : the first step in the distinctly Gothic development of French architecture, according to some recent authorities, is to be found in the apse of the church of Morienval. Morienval is a Romanesque church, but it has ribbed vaulting, of which there is no earlier instance in France. At St. Germer-de-Fly we find the first truly Gothic apse on a large scale ever constructed. It belongs to the second quarter of the twelfth century. The same church possesses a vaulted triforium which may fairly be considered the forerunner of the far grander one at Paris. Again, the now suburban church of St. Denis has double aisles, which clearly foreshadow the noble arrangement which exists at Paris, Amiens, and elsewhere. Many writers are agreed in regarding St. Denis as the starting-point of French Gothic.

Notre Dame was the first of the greater French cathedrals in which Gothic principles of construction were logically carried out. Ths choir was begun, according to M. V. Mortet in his *Etude Historique et Archéologique sur la Cathédrale de Paris*, in the year 1163.[2] The nave (with the exception of the extreme west end) was completed about the year 1195. The west façade was built in the early part of the thirteenth century. Notre Dame is thus older than the cathedral of Amiens, with which one naturally compares it. Amiens was

[1] The difficulty of attributing mediæval work in any countries to particular designers is generally recognised. I do not wish to imply, in the passage to which this note has reference, that the mechanic and the artist were of necessity separate people. Most often the plan was arranged by a master-builder who himself superintended the scheme of decoration.

[2] I give the dates assumed by M. V. Mortet and later writers as well as those affixed by M. Viollet-le-Duc. It will be noticed that the differences between them are not material.

SECTION OF NAVE AND DOUBLE AISLE, AND A PLAN OF ONE BAY.
SCALE 1 INCH = 29 FEET.

(*From Viollet-le-Duc.*)

built between the years 1220 and 1288, except the lower stages of the west front, which were only completed towards the end of the fourteenth century. The towers are a "debased" addition. In England the work being done while the older parts of Notre Dame were in course of erection was transitional; the new style had by no means been fully understood and put into practice. Perhaps we do not over-state the case when we say that the *science* (as well as the art) of Gothic found its first real expression on a large scale in the Cathedral of Paris.

A glance at the ground-plan of Notre Dame shows us how widely it differs from that of our own great churches. First of all we notice that not merely the nave, but the choir, possesses double aisles—a feature which is lacking in English churches [1] on so vast a scale as Canterbury, York, Ely or Peterborough. The magnificence which the system of double aisles lends to a great church need hardly be insisted upon. For a French church the nave of Paris is long, consisting of ten bays. The smaller Norman nave of Norwich possesses, however, no less than fourteen bays. At Paris one is struck by the slight projection of the transepts. In nearly all the greater churches of England the transepts are of large proportions, and frequently (as at Canterbury and Lincoln) we find two pairs of transepts. The transepts at Notre Dame are without aisles, and are so shallow that the church is only just cruciform. Speaking of these transepts Professor Roger Smith observes: "They do not project beyond the line of the side walls, so that, although fairly well marked in the exterior and interior of the building, they add nothing to its floor-space."

The east end of Notre Dame takes the form of a magnifi-cent semicircular apse,—a form assuredly the most appropriate to a Gothic church. The square eastern termination, so common in England, is rare amongst the larger churches of the best period of French Gothic. "A more beautiful eastern termination than the Gothic apse," says Mr. Charles Herbert Moore, [2] "could hardly be conceived. No part of the

[1] Chichester, which is an early church, has double aisles; it is, however, comparatively small, and can in no sense be compared with so immense a building as Notre Dame.
[2] *Development and Character of Gothic Architecture.* Second edition. New York: The Macmillan Company, 1899.

edifice does more honour to the Gothic builders. The low

Photo]   [*Ed. Hautecœur, Paris.*

NORTH AISLES OF THE NAVE.

Romanesque apse, covered with the primitive semi-dome, and enclosed with its simple wall, presented no constructive difficulties, and produced no imposing effect. But the soaring French *chevet*, with its many-celled vault, its arcaded stories, its circling aisles and its radial chapels, taxed the utmost inventive power, and entranced the eye of the beholder." It seems to me that throughout his study of Gothic Mr. Moore is a little less than fair to the Romanesque builders. The Gothic apse, which he so justly admires, is, after all, evolved from the Romanesque apse, which he holds in such light esteem. While we may admit the superiority of the Gothic apse, it is going too far to assert that the Romanesque apse "produces no imposing effect." The apse of Norwich or Peterborough, or of St. Bartholomew's (London) is assuredly imposing in a very high degree.

In a subsequent chapter the structural and decorative details will be fully discussed. It may, however, be noted in passing that, although the Cathedral of Paris is in all essentials a Gothic building, the influence of the Romanesque style is so marked in some of its details that it is frequently described as a transitional structure. As we have seen, the greater part of Notre Dame belongs to the twelfth century ; and De Caumont, who in his *Abécédaire* attempted for French architecture a work of scientific division similar to that which Rickman essayed for English architecture, describes French work of the twelfth century as *Architecture Romane-Tertiaire ou de Transition*. The *Abécédaire*, however, is now considered ingenious rather than authoritative.

With a few words about the west front this brief chapter must be concluded. The great façade of Notre Dame was begun in 1202. It bears a general structural resemblance to that of the cathedral of Senlis, which dates from the second half of the twelfth century, especially in the matter of its triple portals and the towers at the termination of the aisles. At Senlis we have unmistakable evidence of the Gothic spirit, but in its main plan this front is similar to the Romanesque Abbaye-aux-Hommes at Caen. The builders of the west front of Notre Dame thus owe something to the designers of Senlis and the Abbaye-aux-Hommes, but they have achieved a variety and symmetry of which their forerunners probably did not dream. In construction, as well as in the organic significance of its wealth of sculptured decoration, the façade of Notre Dame is genuinely Gothic as opposed to Romanesque.

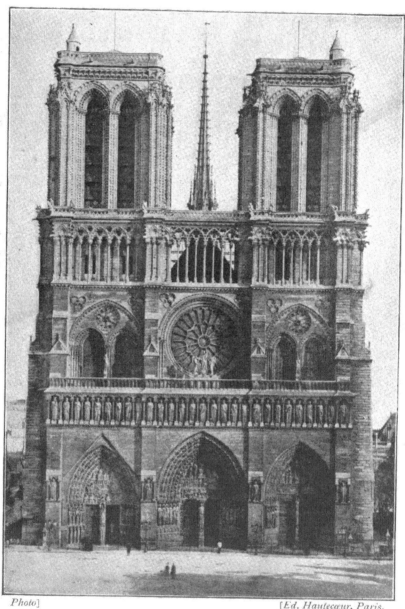

THE WEST FRONT.

CHAPTER III.

Photo]   *[Ed. Haulecœur, Paris.*

CHIMÈRES.

I HAVE already said enough in reference to the commanding position occupied by Notre Dame among the monuments of Paris. The great cathedral seen at a distance looks ancient indeed, but a closer inspection proves to us that the hands of modern men have been at work on it. Indeed, one writer goes so far as to regret that it has been scraped and patched without, and bedizened and bedaubed within. In the first edition of Victor Hugo's famous novel, *Notre Dame*, he tells us that "if we examine one by one the traces of destruction imprinted on this ancient church, the work of time would be found to form the lesser portion—the worst destruction has been perpetrated by men—especially by men of art." Since Hugo wrote this much more "restoration" has been carried out at the metropolitan church of Paris. But though I regret so-called "restoration" on principle, I cannot help feeling that the work executed by M. Viollet-le-Duc and M. Lassus is far less objectionable than it might have been. Fortunately, unlike so many great Continental churches, Notre Dame stands free and clear, and may be examined on all sides without difficulty. Indeed, it is now perhaps somewhat too isolated at the west end. Of course it does not possess one of those venerable closes, with a supplement of ancient ecclesiastical buildings, which is the glory of the great churches of our own land.

The Façade.—The west fronts of the greater Gothic churches of France are as a rule the most majestic features of their exteriors. One might write much to prove that the west front of Amiens or of Chartres is superior to that of Notre Dame, but this, after all, is an arguable question. When we stand in front of the church by the Seine we are struck by the reticence, by the obvious disdain of the easily obtained picturesque, which seem to have animated its designers. The thing is symmetrical with a fine symmetry rare among buildings of the time. Before we discuss the façade in detail, let us quote a translation of Victor Hugo's detailed description, in the romance already alluded to :

"Assuredly there are few finer pages of architecture than this façade, in which, successively and at once, the three receding pointed portals; the decorated and lace-like band of twenty-eight royal niches; the vast central rose window flanked by the two lateral ones, like the priest by the deacon and sub-deacon; the lofty yet slender gallery of trefoiled arcading, which supports a heavy platform upon its light and delicate columns ; and lastly the two dark and massive towers (with their eaves of slate,[1]—harmonious parts of an entirely magnificent whole,—rising one above another in five gigantic stories,—unfolding themselves to the eye combined and unconfused, with innumerable details of statuary and sculpture which powerfully emphasise the grandeur of the *ensemble* : a vast symphony in stone, if one may say so—the colossal work of a man and of a nation . . . on each stone of which one sees, in a hundred varieties, the fancy of the craftsman disciplined by the artist: a kind of human creation, mighty and prolific as the Divine Creation itself of which it seems to have caught the double characteristics—variety, eternity." In the last few phrases Victor Hugo has, perhaps, been guilty of the licence readily granted to so great a master of rhetoric ; but the west front of Notre Dame was a monument certain to

[1] These have been removed.

appeal to a writer to whom none deny the gift of eloquence.
Even a specialist who scrupulously avoids rhapsody is compelled
to use superlatives in his description of this façade : "This
vast and superb design is not only the most elaborate that had
been produced up to its time, but in point of architectural
grandeur it has hardly ever been equalled." Mr. C. H.
Moore, in the book
alluded to in a former
chapter, rightly insists
that the component
elements of the front
are so treated as to
manifest the Gothic
spirit not merely in the
portals, the arcades,
and the apertures, but
even in so comparatively

small a matter as the
profiles of the mould-
ings.

STRING-COURSE ON THE WEST FRONT.
[From Viollet-le-Duc.]

The late P. G. Hamerton has well expressed a feeling
of vague disappointment which many persons who are not
experts in Gothic construction and decoration feel on seeing
the west front : "May I confess frankly," says Mr. Hamerton,
"that until I had carefully studied it under the guidance of
Viollet-le-Duc, the front of Notre Dame never produced upon
me the same effect as the west fronts of some other French
cathedrals of equal rank ? I believe the reason to be that
Notre Dame is not so picturesque as some others, and does
not so much excite the imagination as they do. It is well
ordered, and a perfectly *sane* piece of work (which Gothic
architecture is not always), but it has not the imaginative
intricacy of Rouen, nor the rich exuberance of Amiens and
Reims, nor the fortress-like grandeur of Bourges, nor the
elegant variety of Chartres. . . . The truth is that the
virtues of the west front of Notre Dame are classic rather
than romantic. Everything in it seems the result of perfect
knowledge and consummate calculation. There are none of
those mistakes which generally occur in a work of wilder
genius."

The sculptured decoration of the three great portals exceeds, if not in actual ornateness, at all events in real beauty, that of any cathedral in the west of Europe. Much of it has suffered at the hands of the iconoclast, but, looking to the vicissitudes through which Notre Dame has passed, it is wonderful that so much of the original sculpture has been preserved. The recent restoration has been carried out with

a skill which is simply marvellous, and the uninformed observer may easily be betrayed into the belief that he is looking at an unaltered ancient work. Whether this is a gain or a loss each of us must decide for himself. Some able writers have urged that the success with which ancient work has been imitated shows that modern artists are capable of the triumphs of the middle ages. Others dismiss the new work as an unpardonable forgery. It is outside the scope of this book to attempt to describe in detail the wealth of statuary and carving which the thirteenth-century craftsmen and those of modern times have lavished on these portals. For such a description we must refer the reader to the voluminous accounts of Viollet-le-Duc and other writers. The sculptures of the north door, called the *Portail*

CARVED FOLIAGE FROM THE PORTAIL
DE LA VIERGE.
[*From Viollet-le-Duc.*]

ae la Saint Vierge, have been described as constituting a complete poem in stone. Viollet-le-Duc considered the portal as the masterpiece of French carving of the early thirteenth century. I adapt the following description of the chief sculptures from Mr. Lonergan: On the pedestal of the central pier are bas reliefs representing the Creation of Eve, the Temptation in

PORTAIL DE LA SAINTE VIERGE.

the Garden of Eden, and the Ejection from Paradise. Above
is the Virgin crowned, and over her a small gabled construction

photo 2.

FIGURE OF ST. MARCEL, PORTE SAINTE ANNE.

referring to the Ark of the Covenant. On the upper part
of the arch in the lower division are three prophets and three
kings. In the second angels hold the winding-sheet in which

D

Mary's body lies, near a coffin-shaped tomb. Over this stands Christ with eight apostles. In the third division we see Mary glorified. In the *voussure* are sixty figures of angels, patriarchs, kings and prophets as witnesses of the Virgin's glorification. Under the large statues are medallions referring to incidents in the lives of those represented. Thirty-seven bas reliefs ornament the sides and pillars, amongst them being

Photo]   [*Ed. Hautecœur, Paris.*

THE LAST JUDGEMENT.

(From the central doorway.)

the signs of the zodiac and symbolic representations of the months of the year. The ironwork of the doors of this and of the adjoining portals is of a splendidly elaborate character, due, according to a quaint tradition, to the skill and energy of the devil.

The *Central portal* has suffered more from mutilation than those which are on either side of it. In the eighteenth century the architect Soufflot—a man who was nothing if not "classic"—removed the dividing pier and cut away the lower division of the tympanum in order to facilitate the passage of processions on high ceremonial occasions. All traces of his vandalism have been removed, and the dividing pillar bears a modern statue of Christ by Geoffroy Dechaume. The pedestal is a pentagon, and has seven bas-relief medallions. At the sides are the apostles, while in the medallions are

Photo]　　　　　　　　　　　　　　　　[Ed. Hautecœur, Paris.

TYMPANUM OF THE PORTE SAINTE ANNE.

represented the virtues and vices. Traces of mutilation are apparent in much of this work. The tympanum itself is devoted to the Last Judgment. "First we have figures of the dead rising at the blast of the trumpet. Men and women of all conditions and ranks wearily shake off the sleep of death." Also there is the Archangel, with representations on the right of "the elect joyfully glancing heavenwards, while on the left the grinning demons haul a row of chained souls to hell. Crowning all is seen the Redeemer, showing the wounds in

His hands. Near Him are two angels, and behind the Virgin and St. John the Evangelist interceding on their knees for fallen humanity. As a setting to this magnificent composition

Photo]   [*Ed. Hautecœur Paris.*

APOSTLES.

(From the central doorway.)

are six rows of sculptured forms, making a *voussure* or set of curves, with figures of prophets, doctors, martyrs, devils, toads, damned souls, and a hideous ape with crooked toes and finger-nails. Some of the ornamentation of the six ranges of arch

curves is gruesome and terrible. It relates either to the
celestial or infernal results of the last judgment." In its
original state this great doorway must have been a work of

Photo]   [Ed. Hautecœur, Paris
THE PORTE SAINTE ANNE.
(Figures from the Old Testament)

unrivalled dignity. Nowhere else do we find carving more
expressive, nor more perfectly subordinated to the architectural
scheme.

The doorway on the south is variously described as the

Portal of St. Anne or *St. Marcel.* According to some writers it is the most ancient of the three, and contains fragments of the sculpture which formerly adorned the old church of St. Stephen (St. Etienne). These, it is said, were executed at the expense of Etienne de Garlande, who died in 1142. The dividing pier or *trumeau* bears the statue of St. Marcel (see p. 33). The tympanum is adorned with the " History of Joachim and Anna," the " Marriage of the Virgin," and the " Budding of Joseph's

Photo]   [*Ed. Hautecœur, Paris.*
" CHIMÈRES."

Staff." Each side is occupied with four statues of saints of the Old Testament. The four main buttresses which divide the façade perpendicularly into three parts are pierced with niches containing statues on a level with the vaulting of the portals. These statues represent Religion, Faith, St. Denis, and St. Stephen.

The second story of the façade is occupied by a noble arcade which shelters twenty-eight colossal statues. This is known as *La Galerie des Rois*, and stretches across the entire width of the front. The statues were formerly believed to be conventional representations of the ancient kings of France, but they are doubtless intended for the kings of Judah as ancestors of the Virgin. A similar feature will be found as part of the façade of Amiens. There, however, the statues are at a greater height from the ground, and are twenty-two in number. Above the *Galerie des Rois* at Paris there is a

Photo]　　　　　　　　　　　　　　[*Ed. Hautecœur, Paris.*

" CHIMÈRES."

graceful open arcade of slender arches and columns. The five large statues here date only from the year 1854. The third main division has in the centre a vast wheel window with open tracery, while in each of the lateral bays we have pointed arches with twin pointed openings and small circular panels in the tympanum. The vacant space in the spandrels of each division is occupied by a trefoil panel. At Amiens once more we meet with a main division similarly composed.

At Notre Dame, immediately over the division containing the wheel window, is an open arcaded screen of gigantic proportions, surmounted by a parapet or pierced cornice behind which rise the two towers. So dexterously has this arcade been planned, so graceful are its lines, so delicate its details, that the impression which it leaves on the mind— in spite of the solidity of its construction and the vastness of its scale—is almost that of some such unsubstantial material as lace. To the platform supported by this screen everybody should ascend, if only to make the acquaintance of the famous *Chimères or "Devils of Notre Dame."* This collection of specimens of fantastic sculptured zoology is without parallel in Europe. These weird beasts which scowl from their point of vantage upon the French metropolis fascinated the great etcher Méryon, and more recently they have formed the subject of a series of admirable drawings by Mr. Joseph Pennell, the value of which has been enhanced by an essay, partly descriptive, partly philosophical, from the pen of the late R. A. M. Stevenson. The *chimères* are not merely curious examples of the extravagantly grotesque. Their horror lies, not in their departure from natural forms, but in the fact that, while the features of various beasts or monsters are retained, they are impressed with characteristics of ferocity and cunning which are essentially diabolical or suggestive of the lowest depths of human depravity. They have nothing in common with the crude and impossible gargoyles so frequently found in buildings erected when the pointed style was in its decadance. Speaking roughly, their anatomy is possible : it is conceivable that they should breathe and live.

Readers of Hugo's *Notre Dame* will remember his description of the Archdeacon as he clung to the lead gutter of the tower : "Meanwhile he felt himself going bit by bit; his fingers slipped upon the gutter; he felt more and more the increasing weakness of his arms and the weight of his body ; the piece of lead which supported him inclined more and more down-wards. He saw beneath him, frightful to contemplate, the pointed roof of St. Jean-le-Rond, small as a card bent double. He looked, one after another, at the imperturbable sculptures of the tower—like him suspended over the precipice—but without terror for themselves or pity for him. All around him was stone,—before his eyes the gaping monsters ; in the

"LE STRYGE," ONE OF THE CHIMAERAS OF NOTRE DAME, WITH THE TOWER
OF ST. JACQUES.

(After Méryon's Etching.

Insatiable vampire l'eternelle luxure,
Sur la grande cité convoite sa pâture.

Parvis below, the pavement; above his head, Quasimodo weeping."

The **Towers**, though not of precisely the same size, appear to be so. The summit of the north tower is reached by an ascent of two hundred and ninety-seven steps. Each of the towers is pierced with coupled pointed openings and profusely enriched with mouldings and gargoyles. Both of them terminate with open parapets, the staircases ending in small turrets. The panorama of Paris from the top is magnificent, while the view of Notre Dame itself reveals to the full its structural beauty. Few sights are more impressive than that of the great roof ridge of the church, broken by the graceful modern *flèche*, and ending in the circular *chevet*. From this high place, likewise, one is able fully to appreciate the grand arrangement of flying buttresses, the forest of pinnacles, the host of gargoyles, statues, and other sculptured ornaments which adorn the structure. Of the famous peal of thirteen ancient *bells* which formerly occupied the belfries of the two towers, only one—*le bourdon de Notre Dame*—still remains. It has announced to Paris most of the great victories of the French army, and it still gives the signal to other bells to usher in the great festivals of the Church. Of the other bells existing here, the most interesting is one of Russian workmanship, which was brought from Sebastopol.

The **Flèche**, over the crossing, was built in 1859-60, the ancient one being destroyed in 1787 and replaced by a bulb-like structure which was irreverently compared to a pepper box. To this circumstance Victor Hugo alludes scornfully: "Un architecte de bon goût l'a amputé, et a cru qu'il suffisait de masquer la plaie avec ce large emplâtre de plomb, qui ressemble au couvercle d'une marmite." In removing this atrocity Viollet-le-Duc was assuredly performing a necessary service. His elaborate though slender steeple is of oak covered with lead, and weighs 750,000 kilos. It is ornamented with numberless crockets and pierced with well-contrived openings. The base is led up to by tiers of statues placed on brackets in the angles formed by the junction of the roofs of the nave, transepts and choir. The ball below the cross encloses reputed fragments of the cross and the crown of thorns. There can be little doubt that Viollet-le-Duc, speaking generally, has constructed a flèche which would

THE ROOF-RIDGE OF NOTRE DAME.

(From a drawing by Joseph Pennell, by permission of the " Pall Mall Magazine.")

THE ORIGINAL FLÈCHE.
(*From " Paris à travers les Ages "*)

have commended itself to mediæval designers. It is interesting to note the slender character of the structures which in France rise above the crossings, as compared with the huge towers which occupy a like position in the English cathedrals of Lincoln, Canterbury and York, or with the comparatively substantial spires to be found at Salisbury, Norwich and Lichfield.

The Buttress System. The buttress system of Notre Dame has been the subject of careful study and explanation by Mr. Moore. "In the external system," he remarks, "the flying buttresses were, as at first constructed, magnificently developed, and were double in a twofold sense. That is, the piers which divide the double aisles were formerly carried up through the roof so as to form buttresses to the vaulted triforium gallery, and, rising above the roof of this gallery, they received the heads of the double flying buttresses over the outer aisle, and gave foothold to another pair of arches over the triforium gallery. The lower arch of the outer pair was above the aisle roof, while the lower arch of the inner pair was beneath the roof of the triforium. The principle of equilibrium maintained by opposing thrusts was here completely developed; the inert principle no longer governs the construction, though a survival of the former method of building is found in the walls of the aisles and clerestory, which are no longer necessary to the strength of the edifice."

Photo]   *[Ed. Hautecœur, Paris.*

CLOCHETON OR TURRET—APSIDAL CHAPELS.

The flying buttresses, as we now see them, are (according to Viollet-le-Duc) alterations dating from the early part of the thirteenth century. They consist of huge arches clearing both aisles with a single span. The flying buttresses of the upper tier are wonderfully light and elegant, looking always to the

large span which they have to .clear.   They join the space
between the windows of the clerestory to lofty upright
buttresses terminating in fine crocketed pinnacles and ornamented with an amazing wealth of sculpture.   The flying
buttresses of the lower tier are thicker, and most frequently
spring from elaborate *clochetons*, one of which is illustrated here.

   The Windows of Notre Dame are on the vast scale
which is usual in the greater Gothic churches of the Ile-de-

Photo]   [*Ed Hautecœur, Paris.*
                  WINDOWS ON THE SOUTH SIDE.

France, and present a very remarkable contrast to the small
and simple windows which were deemed sufficient by the
builders of our own early cathedrals in the pointed style.
At Notre Dame the area of solid wall is slight in relation to
the area filled in with glass.   It is not so much a case of
windows in walls, as of walls connecting windows.   The
external buttress system and the internal vaulting system at
Notre Dame comprise the essentials of the structure, so that
the walls are of the nature of enclosures rather than necessary

structural parts. We have travelled far from the Romanesque principle, in which the walls were primarily weight-bearers. The windows of the aisles and of the ambulatory are of great size and display many differences of detail, but they nevertheless maintain a general similarity, the designers, while appreciating the value of uniformity, being too richly endowed with the prevailing fertility of invention in matters of decorative detail exactly to repeat even the most successful arrangement. Each is divided into two main pointed lights, above which a

Photo.]   *[Ed. Hautecœur, Paris.*

TRIFORIUM WINDOWS.

large circle, quatrefoil or similar device, occupies the head of the window, the arches also being cusped or foiled in varying patterns. The main lights are again subdivided into two, with trefoils or quatrefoils in the heads.

Above these noble windows are gabled heads whose sides are enriched with crockets or cusps, their centres being occupied with circular decorative panels, and their angles having small richly carved bosses. Sometimes the canopies consist of beautiful open-work. Everywhere grotesque gargoyles project between them, and the mouldings terminate in corbels in the shape of small, highly wrought human heads. This series of windows emphasises the prodigality with which sculpture in human forms or in the forms of naturalistic or fantastic animals is to be found in nearly all parts of Notre Dame. It is this prodigality, wisely distributed, which places this cathedral in such acute contrast—speaking from the standpoint of the uninitiated observer—to our own early pointed structures. The upper aisle-wall between the lower tier of flying buttresses is in some parts of the building occupied by wheel windows of varied pattern, most elaborately ornamented. But at the east end the triforium lights show another device : two small arches have in the angle between them quatrefoiled openings. It is notable that this dignified and beautiful device is foreshadowed by some of the windows in the Byzantine church in Athens, and even in the sixth-century church of Qualb Louzeh, in Central Syria.

The clerestory lights occupy the full width of the space between the piers of the upper flying buttresses. Finally, at the base of the roof runs an open-work parapet. As we have already observed, many of the windows were hastily rebuilt after the fire of which we have previously spoken.

North and South Transept Fronts.—These, as we have seen, are comparatively late work, but though subordinate to the great façade, they are of intricate design and great ornateness. They fail of effect, however, when they are compared with the monumental and inevitable grandeur of the west front. The south façade, of the date 1257, is undoubtedly the work of Jean de Chelles. An inscription tells us very exactly that it was begun on the second day of the Ides of February, in honour of the mother of Christ. There are writers who would have us believe that to the work of de Chelles we should apply, if not the word "debased," at least the word "flamboyant." For this there seems to be no good reason, unless, indeed, we are prepared to allow that systems of architectural classification are more important than the buildings which are their subject-matter. It will be at once recognised that the lateral fronts of Notre Dame—while they lack the elementary grandeur so conspicuous in the works of the pioneers of Gothic in the Ile-de-France—have nothing in common with the later Perpendicular buildings of England, wherein decoration runs riot

`   [*Ed. Hautecœur, Paris.*

NORTH TRANSEPT FRONT.

E

and construction sometimes degenerates into trickery. The great feature of each of these minor fronts is a vast rose window. It is difficult to repress the feeling that these fronts have been deliberately constructed with a view to lend emphasis to these lovely circular insertions, rich as they are in appropriate tracery. Whether or not we are to limit the work of Jean de Chelles to the southern front (or the lower portion of it), or whether we are to attribute to him the opposite front and the arrangement of chapels adjacent to and east of the transepts, is a nice question. The documentary evidence, to which access is difficult, would, indeed, appear narrowly to limit the work of Jean de Chelles to that fragment with which he has been immemorially associated. But it were unwise to rely too closely on ancient documents in which definite statements of fact are not to be found. It is possible that, even if Jean de Chelles did not personally superintend the erection of the southern front, he designed the opposite front and the chapels in question. He may, indeed, have left pupils fully acquainted with his methods and nearly tied to him by bonds of sentiment, who in their own productions perpetuated, not merely the main features of the style of their master, but used exactly the same material as he employed. Once more, the sculptor is prominent ; once more, the structural parts are adorned with beautiful statuary. The great point is that (using the word as widely as it may fairly be used) uniformity is achieved. Of Notre Dame we may say—what we cannot say of buildings possibly more interesting to the architect and the antiquary—that from east to west, from north to south, it strikes the observer as the splendid outcome of a single imagination, or of a number of imaginations dominated by the same impulse, rather than the haphazard result of peculiar and fortuitous circumstances.

The sculpture of the portal of the North Transept is devoted to the history of the Virgin—of whom the dividing pier between the doors bears a beautiful statue. The carving in the lowest division of the tympanum deals with the Birth of Christ, the Visit of the Magi, the Presentation in the Temple, and the Flight into Egypt. The carving of the other divisions refers to the history of Theophilus, a mythical monk who signed a contract with the Devil, like Faust, but was saved by the interference of the Virgin. On each side of the portal

are three empty niches.   These, as well as the portal, possess
canopies.   An arcade of lights is the chief feature, between

Photo]   [Ed. Haulecœur, Paris

TYMPANIUM OF THE NORTH TRANSEPT DOORWAY.

the entrance and the great rose window previously alluded
to.   The portal of the South Transept has figures of Christ,
St. Martin, St. Stephen, St. John the Baptist, Moses, St. Denis,

St. Thomas, St. Peter, St. Bartholomew, David, and Aaron. *photo 24.*
The tympanum has a representation of the Martyrdom of
St. Stephen. This portal is seldom used. Again we have
the arcade of lights leading to the great rose. The gable
end is in its turn pierced by another smaller circular
window of remarkable beauty. It will be seen that while
there are great differences between the fronts of the two
transepts, structurally they resemble one another.

Returning to the north side of the church, beneath one of
the windows belonging to a choir chapel is the well-known *photo 25*
Porte Rouge, a delicate masterpiece which we may probably
attribute to the early part of the fourteenth century. In its
tympanum is represented the Coronation of the Virgin, while
in its vaulting we have scenes in the life of St. Marcel. The
door gained its name from the fact that it was originally painted
red. It seems always to have held a high place in the
affections of the Parisians. Victor Hugo appears specially
to have delighted in it, for he writes : " La petite Porte-Rouge
atteint presque les limites des délicatesses gothiques du
quinzième siècle." Near the *Port Rouge*, under the windows
of the Choir chapels, are seven bas-reliefs representing scenes *photos*
from the Virgin's life. They date from the sixteenth century. *26, 27.*

He must be insensible indeed to the grandeur of Gothic
building who fails to be impressed when he stands at the
east end of Notre Dame. There, in the great main circular
sweep, we can appreciate the tiers of buttresses, the spear-
like forest of pinnacles, each one constructively necessary,
each duly subordinated to an ordered scheme, each wisely *photo*
and appropriately decorated. Standing here, we are indeed
under the spell of the august *ecclesia parisiaca*, the ancient
silent witness of changes so immense and so fruitful of result,
of victories in the arts alike of peace and war which have
been of such profound consequence not merely to Paris,
and to France, but to mankind in general.

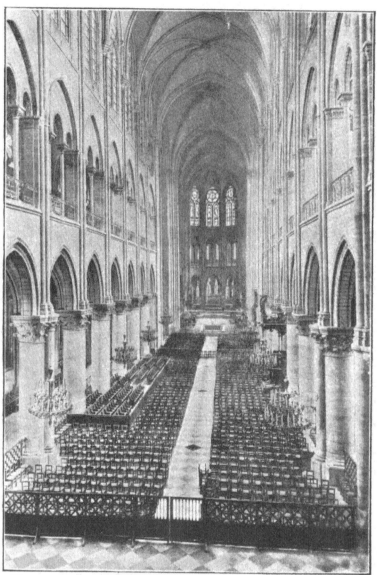

THE INTERIOR FROM THE WEST END.

CHAPTER IV.

THE INTERIOR.—THE NAVE.

IT is difficult accurately to state why a sense of disappointment is so often felt on entering the Cathedral of Paris. The unsatisfactory impression given by Notre Dame is one experienced by visitors of all kinds. The architectural critic, who looks upon a Gothic church as the result of certain clearly defined principles of construction and decoration, must inevitably find in it much to admire. But while it satisfies the specialist, and possibly impresses those who have little pretence to technical information, it lacks the qualities of mystery and of surprise which distinguish some buildings less ancient and less stately. Thus we find one writer complaining that it is heavy, another that it is cold, and a third that it is relatively unpicturesque. Most of those who have recorded their dissatisfaction with the interior of Notre Dame have sought to explain the causes thereof. The splendid promise of the exterior, it is suggested, discounts the remarkable beauties of the inside. Some feel that the regularity, the coherence which distinguish the church, produce an *ensemble* at once ponderous and monotonous. Others complain of the lack of colour ; while on the other hand not a few protest against the intrusion of recent polychromatic decorations. It is possible that the secret lies in certain structural idiosyncrasies. The church is extremely broad in comparison with its length. The bays are so few as to give to the interior an air of undue severity. Fergusson, in his history of architecture, condemns the vaulting ribs as ineffective. The marble pavement is regarded on all hands as a misfortune : nothing could be more tedious or inappropriate. It is, however, to be observed that as one becomes familiar with the interior its shortcomings are forgotten and the dignity of its proportions and details are apprehended more fairly.

Dimensions.—The length of Notre Dame is 390 ft. ; the width at the transepts, 144 ft. ; the length of the nave, 225 ft. ; and the width of the nave (without the aisles), 39 ft. The height of the vaulting is 102 ft.   De Breul, in his *Théâtre des Antiquités de Paris*, mentions a copper tablet which formerly hung against one of the pillars of Notre Dame and gave the dimensions of the cathedral in the following verses :—

> Si tu veux sçavoir comme est ample,
> De Notre-Dame le grand temple,
> Il y a, dans œuvre, pour le seur,
> Dix et sept toises [1] de hauteur,
> Sur la largeur de vingt-quatre,
> Et soixante-cinq sans rebattre,
> A de long aux tours haut montées
> Trente-quatre sont comptées ;
> Le tout fondé sur pilotis,
> Aussi vrai que je te le dis.

The curiosity of these lines excuses the inaccurate statements, comparatively trifling, conveyed in them.   Notre Dame, unlike most mediæval churches on the Continent, is almost painfully clean.   The gaudy shrines which render some of the most splendid of Italian churches almost grotesque are absent from Notre Dame.   The broom and the duster have been too freely used : all that is not appropriate has been too sedulously banished.

In the old floor, amongst a multitude of other interesting memorials of the dead, the tombstones of the following were to be found : Philippe (son of Louis VI. and Archdeacon of Paris) *d.* 1161 ; Prince Geoffrey of England, *d.* 1186 ; Queen Isabelle of Hainault, *d.* 1189 ; the dauphin, Louis (son of Charles VI.), *d.* 1415 ; Louise (mother of François I.,) *d.* 1531 ; and Louis XIII. (his viscera only), 1643.   Amongst the more famous ecclesiastics were the following : Eudes de Sully (1208) ; Etienne II. (1279) ; Cardinal Aymeric de Magnac (1348) ; Bishop Pierre d'Orgemont (1409) ; and Dumoulin, Patriarch of Antioch (1447).   In addition there were three Archbishops of Paris who died during the seventeenth century, and Renaud, Archbishop of Sens (*d.* 1616).   The substitution of squares of marble for the tombstones of these historic personages admits of absolutely no defence.

[1] A "toise" is something over six feet.

Let us now consider the **Roof.** Mr. Charles Herbert Moore thus describes it in his *Development and Character of Gothic Architecture* :—

" Here is a vast nave (completed except the extreme west end by about the year 1196), so admirably roofed with stone that the work has lasted intact for seven hundred years, and will probably, if not wantonly injured, last for centuries to come. These vaults are sexpartite. . . . The diagonal ribs are round-arched, while the transverse and longitudinal ribs are pointed. The intermediate transverse ribs are, however, pointed but slightly ; and to bring their crowns up to the level of the intersections of the diagonals they are considerably stilted. The crowns of the main transverse ribs are a little lower than those of the diagonals, and those of the longitudinals are lower still. The vaults have, therefore, a distinctly domical form. These various adjustments, by greater or less pointing, stilting, and even by the retention of the round arch where it will serve best, exhibit the flexibility of the Gothic system in an interesting and instructive manner." Mr. Moore, after some further details, continues :—" In the vaults of Paris, as in all Gothic vaults, the shells consist of successive courses of masonry which are slightly arched from rib to rib over each triangular cell. The beds of these successive courses are not parallel, but are variously inclined according as the mason found necessary or convenient in developing the concave and winding surfaces engendered by the forms and positions of the ribs to which they had to be accommodated. These courses of masonry have here in Paris, as they have in most Gothic vaults, a considerable inclination near the springing from the longitudinal rib upward toward the diagonal, and they become gradually more level as they approach the crown of the vault, where they are more nearly parallel. But perfectly parallel they can hardly ever be, since each course forms a portion of a surface that is concaved in all directions." Mr. Moore adds that in the earliest and finest Gothic vaultings this masonry is composed of small stones perfectly faced and closely jointed ; and the vaulting of Paris, especially that of the choir, is a model of careful and finished workmanship.

The vaulting of the choir differs from that of the nave, but the difference is one rather of detail than of principle. We have already said much about the external buttress

system by which this splendid roof is sustained. Internally
this vaulting rises from slender shafts springing from the

Photo]   [*Ed. Hautecœur, Paris.*
THE NAVE : SOUTH ARCADE.

capitals of the great cylindrical columns constituting the main
arcade of the ground story. The piers at Paris are ill
adjusted to the vaults, a feature which has resulted in an

immense amount of learned discussion. They were obviously intended for quadripartite vaulting. It seems probable that suddenly, for a reason which we are not now in a position to appreciate, the quadripartite form was abandoned in favour of the sexpartite form actually adopted. Students of this subject are advised to refer to pp. 114-15 of the second edition of Mr. Moore's book, where the differences between the vaulting imposts of the nave and choir are discussed and delineated. They may profitably compare this with M. Viollet-le-Duc's *Construction* (p. 164). M. Viollet-le-Duc, it may be added, suggests that the necessities of the sexpartite system were provided for by the monolithic shafts grouped round every other pier in the arcade dividing the aisles.

CAPITAL IN THE NAVE.
From Viollet-le-Duc.

The somewhat heavy character of the great cylindrical piers which divide the nave from the aisles is largely redeemed by the beautiful carving with which the capitals are ornamented. The plants which the sculptors have conventionalised are those commonly found in the fields adjacent to Paris. These ornate capitals are genuinely Gothic in feeling, and have nothing in common with those which crown the piers of our Anglo-Norman (Romanesque) cathedrals. Again, the plinths of the columns are utterly unlike the simple and massive bases on which the round columns of our older churches most often rest. We have already alluded to the ill-adaptation of these piers and their capitals to the sexpartite form of vaulting employed. In the case of the most westerly piers of the main arcade an attempt seems to have been made—with no great success, as it appears to me—to minimise the illogical effect of the vaulting imposts. The result has been the emphasis of that very want of congruity which it was sought to remedy. It would be difficult to find a less

satisfactory arrangement than that which obtains in the pier
and capital delineated in our illustration, where four smaller
cylinders are attached to the main one. Here, not merely
is the pier itself rendered unwieldy by its satellites, but the
capital loses all symmetry owing to the interposition of the
small capitals which crown those satellites. It will be noticed
that the arches of the main arcade are by no means uniform.
Thus we have a wide arch adjacent to an extremely narrow
one, while the builders of the period did not hesitate to make
use of a round arch where they found that form more
convenient. It is in some measure these peculiarities which
have induced not a few authors to describe Notre Dame as
a transitional church.

In no part of Notre Dame do we more perfectly appreciate
the grandeur of the scale of the church than when we stand
in the vast double aisles on either side of the nave. With
every step we take the view changes. We hesitate to leave
the spot upon which we stand lest we should lose its charm,
and yet we feel that probably a vista even more beautiful
awaits us a few paces beyond. The lines of vast piers seem
as if they were consciously engaged in surprising us : now
they come together and close the view suddenly, unexpectedly ;
then they open, revealing a richly furnished altar in, as it were,
a colossal frame of masonry. Everywhere the lines of the
building strike us as vast, massive, almost elemental, but
everywhere there is an ordered, if a somewhat ponderous
symmetry. It is strange that there ever was an age in which
the innate dignity and majesty of these lines were not felt. Yet
so barbarous did the architecture of Notre Dame appear to
eighteenth-century eyes, that a desperate attempt was made
to hide it. Vast pictures in gilt frames were placed from
capital to capital of the main arcade on both sides. In this
way the arches were completely hidden, and a square appearance (supposed to suggest the classical) was given to the
lowest story. The openings of the triforium were spared,
as anything placed in front of them would block the view
of the crowds who used to fill the *tribunes* on state occasions.
The nave, however, thus turned into a kind of picture gallery,
was considered very satisfactory (see illustration, p. 11)
Needless to say, no trace of the pictures now remains, and
the great arches are free and open once more. The piers

dividing the aisles are not all of the same construction. Round every other pier are grouped monolithic shafts, possessing delicately foliated capitals with moulded abaci. Two

Photo]   [*Ed Hautecœur, Paris.*
THE NAVE, NORTH ARCADE.

shafts, with a single abacus and plinth, alternate with a single shaft. In all there are twelve shafts round the pier. These piers, with their cluster of satellites, contrast finely with the simple cylinders with bold foliated capitals with which they alternate, and lend variety and interest to the arcades (see illustration, p. 23).

The vaulting of the aisles is quadripartite, the ribs being strongly marked and possessing carved bosses at the point of intersection. Beyond the outer aisles on each side is a series of chapels, which will be described presently. The accompany-ing illustrations give a good idea of the piers, capitals and vaulting of this part of the church.

The Triforium, to which there are four staircases, is of immense size, owing to the fact that it passes over the double aisles on both sides of the nave. Its designers no doubt contemplated its use as a gallery from which the grand ceremonies which took place in the church could be witnessed by large numbers of people. It is ceiled with stone—a feature common to most of the greater cathedrals of France—so that no wooden beams can be seen anywhere in the building. This obviously increases the massiveness of the whole, though a certain tendency to heaviness is perhaps emphasised. The masonry is everywhere very fine, and in the small details a high degree of wise as opposed to futile finish is maintained throughout. The galleries are excellently lighted. Above the nave-aisles low pointed arches enclose a foliated circle, the corners at the base being filled with small trefoils. In the choir the lights consist of rose or wheel windows, in the tracery of which there is great variety of pattern. The openings towards the church take their place admirably in the elevation, being in character with the main arcade beneath and the clerestory above. They are almost austerely simple, and possess none of the ornateness which characterises the triforiums of Westminster, Lincoln, and other English buildings of slightly later date. A large plain pointed arch encloses two and in some cases three pointed arches, which are separated from one another by delicate columns bearing foliated capitals with square abaci. They have small square bases. These columns are a hundred and four in number. A low openwork railing of iron fills in the front of the gallery. The triforium goes round the whole building : that portion which is at the end of the transepts, however, consists of a narrow passage which is not open to the church. The banners which were captured by French armies were exhibited from the triforium so long as war continued. On the conclusion of peace, they were

THE TRIFORIUM GALLERY, OR "TRIBUNES."

(*From "Paris à travers les Ages."*)

taken down—a proceeding which might be followed in other
countries with advantage. The part of the triforium in the

choir differs only in detail from that in the nave. Over the triforium come the vast windows, altered in the thirteenth century, which comprise the **Clerestory,** of which more is said on page 72. The stained glass will be fully discussed hereafter.

The upper portion of the west end is filled by the great rose window, which, as we have noticed, is so beautiful a feature of the façade. The tops of the pipes of the great organ hide the lower part of it from our view inside. The lovely painted glass, which is ancient, has representations of the Virgin and Child surrounded by prophets. Amongst other features are the signs of the Zodiac, the labours of the months, and the Virtues in triumph with lances in their hands. The gallery on which the organ is now placed was possibly used for the performance of miracle plays.· As it is at a relatively great height from the pavement, this is at least doubtful. The **Organ** is a fine instrument of wonderful power. It was practically rebuilt by Thierry Lesclope in 1730, and enlarged by Cliquot in 1785. In recent years it has been immensely improved by M. Cavaillé-Coll, who gave it 5266 pipes and 80 stops. It plays a great part in the splendid musical services for which the Cathedral is famous.

The Nave is almost devoid of monuments; nothing breaks up the vast lines of the architecture. The most important tomb is that of Jean Etienne Yver, Canon of Paris and Rouen, who died in February 1467. It has escaped serious mutilation, and is a realistic performance in the style prevailing in France at the end of the fifteenth century. On the base is a gruesome representation of the body of the Canon being given over to the worms. Above this, two saints are helping him to rise from the coffin, and directing his attention towards Heaven. The whole thing is repulsive, but it is interesting as a curiosity. Many historic memorials perished during the Revolution, but some were removed to Versailles and still exist there. They include the tombs of Jean Jouvenel des Ursins (d. 1431) and his wife Michelle de Vitry ; the Maréchal Albert de Gondi, Duc de Retz (d. 1602) ; and his brother Pierre de Gondi, Bishop of Paris (d. 1616). Two monuments have disappeared from the nave which were highly esteemed in their day. Writing of Notre Dame in his *Crudities* in 1611, Thomas Coryat says: "I could see no notable matter in the cathedrall church, saving the statue of Saint Christopher on the right hand at the coming in of the great gate, which is indeed very exquisitely done, all the rest being but ordinary."

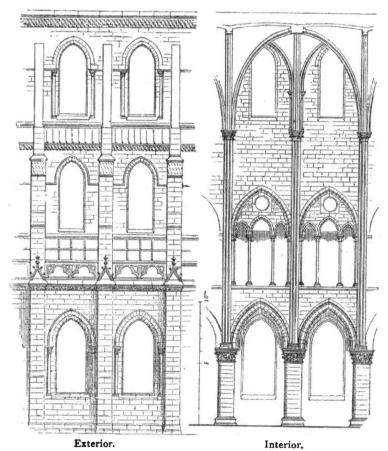

Exterior.   Interior.

ELEVATIONS OF THE NAVE.

(*From Viollet-le-Duc.*)

The statue so delighted the old traveller that he had eyes for nothing else, for the architecture of Notre Dame is anything but ordinary. The Chapter of the Cathedral did not share his

F

view, for they deliberately destroyed it in 1786. It was
presented to the church in 1413 by Antoine des Essarts,
whose tomb with his effigy in armour stood near it. Its
destruction is remarkable, for colossal things were very much
to the taste of those who lived at the end of the seventeenth
century. The Revolution is responsible for the destruction of
a famous equestrian statue which stood in the nave until
1792. It is generally considered to have been that of
Philippe le Bel, clothed in the armour in which he won his
victory over the Flemings at Mons-en-Pucelle in 1304. The
identity of the statue has, however, been the subject of
controversy. Viollet-le-Duc tells us that it represented, not
Philippe le Bel, but Philippe VI. (of Valois), who defeated the
Flemings at Cassel in 1328. On his return to Paris he rode
into the cathedral on horseback in state, and vowed his
harness to the Virgin. The Chapter disagree with Viollet-le-
Duc, who is, however, supported in his contention by the
Benedictine Père Montfaucon, by the writers who continued
the chronicle of William of Nangis, and some others. The
monument stood close to the last pillar on the right side of
the nave. The **Pulpit** is a modern work, after the design
of Viollet-le-Duc. It is of oak, and its decorations include
statues of six of the apostles and of angelic figures. Suspended
from the vaulting are eight imposing candelabra in bronze-
gilt.

The Chapels of the Nave contain singularly few features
of historic interest, nor amongst the furniture of their altars are
there many recent works of art of outstanding merit. They
introduce us, however, to the vast scheme of mural painting
which has been carried out from the designs and partly under
the direction of Viollet-le-Duc. There can be no doubt
that some scheme of polychromatic decoration was legitimate :
almost every ancient church in France has indisputable evidence
of its employment in the middle ages. The problem which
faced Viollet-le-Duc was one of extreme difficulty. The area
to be covered was enormous : the variations of light were
excessive. Some parts were luminous, even radiant ; others
were hidden in almost continuous gloom. The schemes of
colour had to be adapted to these varying conditions. The
use of mosaic was considered and discarded. The expense
would have been gigantic, and the material was considered,

perhaps rightly, to be inappropriate to the style of architecture. Wall pictures, as such, were regarded as destructive to the *ensemble*, fatiguing to the eyes and mind, and productive of a certain patchy effect. A series of symbolical patterns of a rigidly conventional type, in which human figures are very sparingly used, was devised. It may be admitted at once that the learning and ingenuity displayed in the design of the scheme were such as might be expected from the most erudite and accomplished French architectural scholar of our time. The minute consideration which Viollet-le-Duc devoted to the subject may be judged from the following passage : "D'abord, la cathédrale de Paris, comme on sait, est orientée de telle façon que tout un côté du monument se présente vers le midi et l'autre vers le nord. Un de ces côtés reçoit donc une lumière plus vive et plus colorée que l'autre. Il a paru qu'il était nécessaire de profiter de cette disposition pour établir l'harmonie générale. Au lieu de combattre l'effet de cette orientation, on a cru devoir l'appuyer. Ainsi, en premier lieu, toutes les fenêtres des chapelles tournées vers le sud sont garnies de grisailles à tons nacrés et froids. De là il resulte qu'en entrant dans le monument on voit un côté de lumière, un côté d'ombre, un côté chaud et brillant et un côté froid. Il en résultei nstinctivement pour l'œil un effet général tranquille. Rien n'est plus fatigant pour les yeux qu'un intérieur éclairé par les jours contraires de qualités semblables comme intensité de lumière, valeur de tons et coloration. La peinture des chapelles devait concorder naturellement avec le système de répartition de la lumière. Suivant une règle générale, la tonalité des peintures du côté nord est plus froide que celle du côté du midi. Cependant, comme il faut conserver l'unité, de distance en distance, du côté sud, des tons gris, des tons verts, froids, rappellent l'harmonie générale du côté nord ; et, du côté septentrional, des tons chauds rappellent l'harmonie générale du côté méridional." [1]

In spite of all these elaborate precautions, in spite of so much patience and learning, the result as a whole seems to me unsatisfactory. One wearies of the ingenious geometrical

[1] "Peintures Murales des Chapelles de Notre-Dame de Paris." Paris : A. Morel. See the preface by Viollet-le-Duc for further details of his principles of decoration.

curves, the crosses, the squares, the lozenges, the coloured stars, the excessively and laboriously conventionalised foliage, . and the rest. The whole strikes one as dead and mechanical, as mere covering of stone for the sake of doing so. And the colour, though by no means aggressive, is unsatisfying. The experiment was heroic, and the result might certainly have been very much worse, but the stone-work would have been better untouched.

The Chapels on the north side of the nave (from west to east) are : 1. The *Chapelle des Fonts Baptismaux.* The bronze carving of the font is by Brachelet. 2. The *Chapelle Saint-Charles.* There are a statue in painted stone by M. de Chaume and a good piscina. The wall decorations are cold and sombre. 3. The *Chapelle de la Sainte-Enfance.* It contains a group representing Christ caressing a French and a Chinese child, by M. de Chaume. 4. The *Chapelle Saint-Vincent-de-Paul.* The decorations of this chapel are somewhat elaborate, and gilding is freely used. 5. The *Chapelle de Saint-François-Xavier.* There is a group representing the Saint baptising a Chinese. 6. *Chapelle de Saint-Landry*, with statue by De Chaume. 7. *Chapelle de Sainte-Clotilde*, with statue by the same artist.

The following are on the south side (west to east) :

1. *Chapelle des Ames du Purgatoire.* Christ rescuing a soul from Purgatory. A statue by De Chaume in coloured stone. The colour scheme of the chapel is warm and brilliant. 2. *Chapelle de Sainte-Geneviève.* The decorations, which are somewhat profuse, were given by the " dames de l'Institut de l'œuvre de Sainte Geneviève." 3. *Chapelle Saint-Joseph*, with statue of Joseph with the Child Jesus in his arms. 4. *Chapelle Saint-Pierre.* Statue in wood of the saint by M. Corbon. The carved woodwork of the sixteenth century still remains, and includes panels with representations of the Twelve Apostles, St. Germain, and Sainte Geneviève. 5. *Chapelle Saint-Anne.* 6. *Chapelle du Sacré-Cœur.* Statue in coloured stone by M. de Chaume. 7. *Chapelle de l'Annonciation.* With a statue of the Virgin in wood by M. Corbon. Paintings by Perrodin, one of the best pupils of Flandrin, of David, St. Michel, Isaiah, St. Anne, St. Joseph, St. John, St. Luke, St. Augustine, St. Bernard, St. Dominic, and St. Bonaventure.

Before we turn from the nave to the choir and transepts, let us say a few words as to the *stained glass*, which was once the glory of the church. There is probably no Gothic interior in France which has suffered more terribly from the destruction of its ancient windows than Notre Dame. The coldness and severity which the mural decorations of Viollet-le-Duc vainly strive to mitigate were perhaps not felt at all when the light from every window seemed to be transmitted in glowing and gleaming shafts of every conceivable colour and tone. Fortunately, the old glass still remains in the great rose windows. That over the west door has been described; the others will be noticed in the account of the transepts. The rest of the glass was deliberately destroyed, not by an infuriated mob, but by those in authority, in 1741.

The work of destruction was performed by Jean Leviel and his brother, who cheerfully substituted for the priceless material they removed great sheets of dull, monotonous *grisaille*, with borders ornamented with the *fleur-de-lis*. The introduction of *grisaille* has been quaintly described by Michelet as *le protestantisme entrant dans la peinture*. Its use at Notre Dame is nothing short of a disaster. Efforts have been made in some parts of the building to replace it with glass of a less sombre character, but these efforts so far have done little to lessen our regret for the calamity of 1741.

Photo]   [Ed. Hautecœur, Paris.

ANGLE OF THE CHOIR AND SOUTH TRANSEPT.

CHAPTER V.

THE austere character of the nave emphasises the splendid decorations of the eastern parts. No massive screen prevents our seeing the church from the great entrance to the apse. The fact that the choir is open possibly lessens our sense of mystery and of awe, but we are more than compensated by the splendid view of the building from end to end.

The irritating custom of railing off the eastern limb of the church and demanding a fee for admission happily does not obtain at Notre Dame. It is all but universal in England, and renders an intelligent appreciation of the architectural history of our great churches a matter of some difficulty. At Paris one may wander where one will, so long as one does not interrupt the offices. That pompous and irresponsible chatterer the cathedral verger does not impose himself upon us, and disturb our study and diminish our pleasure, as he does in churches on this side the Channel. Only the Sacristy need be visited in the company of an official.

The transepts of French cathedrals are rarely such important features as they are in those of this country. The vast church of Bourges has no transepts at all. At Noyon, as at Paris, the transepts have no aisles. Of the crossing and transepts at Paris Viollet-le-Duc and Guilhermy write as follows :

" At the four angles of the crossing, massive piers, some covered with combined pilasters, others with clustered columns, rise without a break from the ground to the vaulting. The two transepts at the outset were only of two bays similar to those of the nave. They were lengthened by a shallower bay when the façades were rebuilt. The later bays are easily distinguished from the four older ones. Thin round vaulting-ribs cross at a crown deeper and more pronounced than those of the older parts. The north and south doors are set in a rich arcading, of which the divisions and the tympanums can be compared to nothing more fitly than a large window with mullions. In the south transept, statues more or less mutilated, representing Christ and the saints, remain at the points of the gables. In describing the exterior of the façades we pointed out the open gallery which extends the whole breadth of each transept, and the great rose window a little above it. The exterior arcading of the gallery is repeated by a similar arcading inside. There is a passage between the two rows of little columns, and there is another above this. The effect of the rose windows in the interior, with glowing stained glass in all their compartments, recalls the marvellous descriptions that Dante has given us of the circles of Paradise. The incomparable splendour alternately astonishes and enchants us. To decorate the side walls of his bays, Jean de Chelles continued the arcading and the mullioned windows."

The vaulting and the rose of the south transept were repaired between the years 1725 and 1728 by Boffrand, the king's architect, at the expense of Cardinal de Noailles. The pair of arches leading to the choir aisles with their elaborate crocketed canopies are somewhat feebly contrived in both transepts. The clustered shafts are clumsily arranged. The details on the north side differ from those on the south. On the east and west sides of both transepts there are two narrow bays of the triforium. The clerestory consists of short pointed windows with wheel windows beneath them. This is due to Viollet-le-Duc, and is intended to show us the arrangement which obtained throughout the church previous to the alterations which resulted from the fire in the thirteenth century.[1]

At the angle of the south transept in front of the great south-east pier of the crossing is the famous statue of the

[1] In his "Paris" (London, Edward Arnold, 1900), Mr. Hilaire Belloc thus refers to the fire of 1218: "In 1218 a happy accident gave us the incomparable unity which the Cathedral alone possesses among mediæval monuments ; for in that year, on the eve of the Assumption, four inspired thieves climbed into the roof-tree and warily let down ropes with slip-knots to lasso the silver candlesticks on the altar. These they snared, but as they pulled them up the lights set fire to the hangings that were stretched for the feasts, and the fire spread to the whole choir." The writer gives no authority for this story.

Virgin and Child, which, in Notre Dame, occupies a place
not unlike the far more famous and more venerable statue of *phot 2*

Photo]   *[Ed. Hautecœur, Paris.*

THE NORTH TRANSEPT.

S. Peter in the vast basilica which at Rome is dedicated to
him. Mr. Belloc has used a photograph of it as the frontispiece

to the volume quoted in the footnote, and he writes of it as follows : " But of all the additions to the interior of Notre Dame which popular fancy or the traditions of some crisis give it, none is more worthy of being known than that which alone survives of them, and which I have made the frontispiece of this book. It is not that the statue has—as so much of the fourteenth century can boast—a peculiar beauty ; it is indeed (when seen from below, as it was meant to be) full of a delicacy that the time was adding to the severity of the thirteenth century ; it has from that standpoint a very graceful gesture ; the exaggeration of the forehead disappears, the features show the delicate and elusive smile that the fourteenth century always gave to its Madonnas, and there appears also in its general attitude the gentle inclination of courtesy and attention that was also a peculiar mark of a statuary which was just escaping the rigidity of Early Gothic. But its beauty, slight and ill-defined, is not, I repeat, the interest of the statue. It is because this image dates from the awakening of the capital to its position in France, because it is the symbol of Paris, that it rises up alone, as you may see it now, where the southern transept comes into the nave,[1] all lit with candles and standing out against the blue and the lilies. It is a kind of core and centre to the city, and is, as it were, the genius catching up the spirit of the wars, and giving the generation of the last siege and reconstruction, as it will give on in the future to others in newer trials, a figure in which all the personality of the place is stored up and remembered. It was made just at the outbreak of the Hundred Years' War, it received the devotion of Etienne Marcel, it heard the outcry that followed the defeat of Poictiers and the captivity of the king." Mr. Belloc concludes : " It has been for these five hundred years and more the middle thing, carrying with full meaning the name ' Our Lady of Paris,' which seems to spread out from it to the Church, and to overhang like an influence the whole city, so that one might wonder sometimes as one looked at it whether it was not the figure of Paris itself one saw."

In front of the statue is an iron grille terminating in spikes for candles. After Poitiers, the citizens of Paris annually offered a gigantic candle to be burned in front of this statue

[1] See p. 70.

in order that the ills which afflicted France might cease. It was of the exact length of the walls of the capital itself, and was of course coiled up ropewise. The first presentation was made on August 14th, 1437. The candle necessarily grew with every increase in the area of the city. By the beginning of the seventeenth century it was felt that the limits of vastness had been reached, and in 1605 a silver lamp, which was always to burn before the statue, was presented instead of the candle. This was destroyed by the Revolutionists. On the pillar below the statue is a sculpture said to represent Eve with the serpent's tail. The identity of the existing statue with the original one so eloquently described by Mr. Belloc has been doubted, but the grounds for doubt appear to be small. In this transept are two marble slabs in memory of seventy-five victims of the Commune.

The place on the north side, corresponding with the statue of Notre-Dame de Paris on the south, is filled by a statue of St. Denis, a fairly good work by Nicolas Coustou.[1] The splendid glass of the great rose window in the south transept has in the main divisions of its four circles the twelve apostles, and a host of bishops and saints with symbols and palms, to whom angels bear golden crowns of glory. In one of the small compartments St. Denis is represented carrying his head, and in others are scenes from what is known as " les Combats des Apôtres," amongst them being the arrival of St. Matthew in the presence of the King of Egypt, and the baptism of the King after his conversion by the Apostle. The great rose window of the opposite transept is devoted to scenes from the life of the Virgin. She is represented with Christ in her arms, and is surrounded with an army of patriarchs, judges, prophets, priests and kings, all of whom are related to the Saviour by ties of blood or as His spiritual forerunners. The glass includes curious representations of the Antichrist, decapitating Enoch ; and of the destruction of the Antichrist by the Almighty, who appears in a cloud. The small rose or wheel windows in the sides of the transepts have been filled with glass from designs by Steinheil. The pavement of the transepts is of squares of black Bourbon marble alternating with Dinan stone. Great attention was given by Viollet-le-Duc to the polychromatic decoration of the transepts,

[1] See p. 89.

but it cannot be said that he has been more successful in these parts of the church than elsewhere. The effect aimed at appears to have been that of tapestry with simple patterns; indeed, of the whole it is said, "cette décoration forme, jusque sous les roses, une sort de brillante tapisserie." Some of the canopies are of the most intricate patterns, but they would be better suited to wood or metal work than to painting. The scheme includes a series of paintings by Perrodin of persons distinguished in the history of the diocese of Paris. The figures have elaborate decorative borders.

The removal of statues and memorials from the nave, which we have already deplored, had just the shadow of a justification from the purely æsthetic standpoint. Many of the monuments were incongruous, some were positively grotesque. In Westminster Abbey we have an example of the shocking effect of inappropriate statuary in a Gothic building; we know, only too well, how terribly one of the most beautiful interiors in the world suffers from a crowd of tombs which are out of keeping with the very spirit of the place. By the removal of the memorials at Notre Dame, the church has doubtless regained the aspect intended by its designers.

The nave leads uninterruptedly to the choir, which ends in the high altar; and the high altar, with the adjacent shrine of St. Marcel, was the primary reason of the existence of the cathedral. We have seen that in its earlier form little or no provision was made for chapels and consequently for side altars. Everything was arranged to concentrate the eye on the chief altar, and to lend dignity to its position. Its sacred character was respected even in the far-off days in which the body of the church was used for commercial purposes, or for festivals the reverse of religious.

The great eastern limb of the church is raised above the transepts by three steps. Once we have passed into the **Ambulatory**, or *pourtour*, of the choir, we are in the most interesting part of the building; for here our story is of historical monuments and decorative objects still happily existing, and not an account of things which have long since ceased to be. When we step into the ambulatory, we pass from newer to older work, but we experience no violent transition from one style to another. The style of the choir is, speaking generally, the style of the whole church. The differences, interesting as they are to the minute student of architectural development, are such as would remain unnoticed by those who do not pretend to special knowledge. This unity reminds one of an Italian Romanesque basilica rather than a Gothic cathedral. Viollet-le-Duc has noted that the capitals in the triforium of the choir seem to be earlier in date than those of the main arcade beneath it ; that if nothing were left save the capitals of the two parts, one would conclude that those of the triforium were earlier. This is manifestly impossible, but it shows that not the smallest deviation of style was allowed in constructing the upper story.

Among the capitals of the columns in the choir there are a few representations of animal life amongst the conventional foliage, while the capitals in the nave represent foliage alone. The choir is throughout a shade nearer Romanesque than the nave, but the difference is so slight that only close examination reveals it. Already we have remarked on the superiority of an apsidal termination to any other form in a Gothic church. The ordered grandeur of Notre Dame is nowhere more impressive than in the beautiful sweep of the apse with its spacious ambulatory. It must have been even more imposing in its simplicity before the construction of the side chapels was undertaken, although we are far from regretting an addition which, though it may have reduced the original dignity of the church, has added variety to it and rendered it more interesting.

Let us begin our detailed examination of the choir and its chapels with the famous **Screen** of sculptures by Jehan Ravy and his nephew Jehan le Bouteiller, which we must study from the ambulatory. In his *History of Sculpture*, Professor Wilhelm Lübke devotes considerable space to this series in the chapter devoted to "Northern Sculpture in the Late Gothic Epoch" (1300 to 1450). After stating that France exhausted herself during the golden age of Gothic sculpture, and that the period under discussion was so stormy as to be unfavourable to the production of works of art, he writes of the screen as follows :

"One of the most important works of the epoch [the end of the thirteenth and the beginning of the fourteenth centuries] are the extensive reliefs which cover the choir screen in the interior of the Cathedral of Paris. These are only the remains of the formerly far richer plastic ornament which, in a great measure, fell a sacrifice under Louis XIV. to a vain love of ostentation. The earlier series on the north side contains a crowded representation in an unbroken line of the History of Christ; from the Annunciation to the Prayer at Gethsemane. These representations are vividly conceived, and the style in which they are executed breathes the spirit of the thirteenth century. Perhaps they belong to the end of that century or to the beginning of the next. The reliefs on the south side are different in many points. They continue the History of Christ; and, indeed, the whole was so arranged that the cycle which began at the east passed along the north side to the west end of the choir, and was continued on the lectern,[1] where the Passion, Crucifixion and Resurrection were depicted in front of the congregation, concluding at the south side in a scene moving from west to east. Of the latter scenes, the only ones now in existence are those which extend from the Meeting of Christ as the Gardener with Mary Magdalen to the Farewell to the Disciples after the Resurrection. The artist of these later scenes left his name, in an inscription that has now disappeared,[2] as Jehan Ravy, who for twenty-six years conducted the building of Notre Dame, at the end of which time it was completed under his nephew Master Jehan de Bouteiller, in 1351. Master Ravy evidently thought that he could improve upon his predecessor's work on the north side; for while the latter had combined the scenes into one unbroken series, he divided his into separate compartments by arcades, so that these later representations, which are still in existence, are separated from each other by small columns. In so doing he followed the general taste of the century, which was inclined to exchange a picturesque character for the calm epic relief of the former period. While, however, his somewhat short figures are certainly superior in correctness to the figures of the north side, owing to his understanding of the physical structure and to the neatness of execution, there is in the figures of the north side a fresher tone of feeling and more grace of action, compared with which the far more constrained

---

[1] The Rood-loft.
[2] This has been restored, and reads: " C'est maistre Jehan Ravy maçon de Notre Dame par Vespace XXV ans qui commença ces nouvelles histoires, et Jehan le Bouteiller son nepveu qui les aparfaites en MCCCLI."

attitudes of the later works form an unpleasing contrast, and even occasionally degenerate into commonplaceness. Thus in these works, in spite of all expenditure of artistic care, there is an unmistakable decline of creative power."

The series on the north side should be visited first. The scenes are fourteen in number, and have reference to the Visitation :

The Shepherds and the Star of Bethlehem ;
The Nativity ;
The Visit of the Magi ;
The Slaughter of the Innocents ;
The Flight into Egypt ;
The Presentation in the Temple ;
Christ among the Doctors ;

His Baptism ;
The Marriage-Feast at Cana ;
The Entry into Jerusalem ;
The Last Supper ;
Christ Washing the Feet of St. Peter ;
The scene in the Garden of Olives ;

The later works on the south side, in which Professor Lübke traces a decline of creative force, represent :

The Meeting of Christ as the Gardener with Mary Magdalen ;
The Holy Women (the Three Maries) Kissing the Saviour's Feet ;
Jesus appearing to the Apostles (who are represented in a turreted building) ;
The Disciples of Emmaus, with Christ among them ;

The Breaking of the Bread ;
Another version of Christ Appearing to the Apostles ;
The Doubt and the Conversion of St. Thomas ;
The Miraculous Draught of Fishes, Christ's Message to the Apostles to Preach the Gospel to all Nations.

It is extremely fortunate that these very interesting sculptures have been left to us, for they constitute incomparably the most important of the internal decorations at Notre Dame, which, as we have seen, is relatively poor in the mediæval tombs which are the glory of Westminster Abbey. While we are thankful for what is left, we cannot help feeling a grudge against Cardinal de Noailles, who caused some of the scenes to be removed, and thus left the series incomplete. That the modern restoration of the painting of the sculpture was wise can hardly be maintained.[1]

For the moment we will leave the ambulatory, and consider

[1] The fine collection of casts at the Crystal Palace includes most of this series. It is a pity that they cannot be placed in some more appropriate and convenient place.

VIEW OF THE CHOIR AT THE END OF THE XIII. CENTURY, SHOWING
THE CARVED ROOD-SCREEN AND THE SHRINE OF ST. MARCEL.

(From Viollet-le-Duc.)

the **Choir and Sanctuary**. It will be interesting, before
we examine the present state of these parts, to sketch briefly
their aspect in the fourteenth century.   Corrozet and De
Breul have left us descriptions which have been illustrated
and elucidated by the indefatigable Viollet-le-Duc.   The
entrance to the choir at the crossing was filled by a magnificent
screen of stone richly adorned with carving. This was about
eighteen feet high. The top formed the rood-loft, which was
approached by two circular staircases placed at either end of
the screen.   In the centre was, of course, the entrance to
the choir. When the doors were open the high altar could
be seen from the end of the nave. Over this door was a
decorated gable terminating in a great crucifix.   According to
De Breul this crucifix was a masterpiece of sculpture, as were
the other statues which composed the group.   The loft was
broad, and had on both sides an open stone parapet, on which
were placed carved lecterns. The west front of the screen
had sculptured scenes of the Passion, which formed part of
the series by Jehan Ravy and Jehan de Bouteiller lately described. On either side of the doorway, beneath the sculptures,
were small altars. The choir-stalls of carved wood occupied
much the same place as do those which we see to-day.
Between the rows of stalls were low tombs with recumbent
figures. The Sanctuary, approached by steps, was railed off,
and filled the apse. The space between the columns was
filled by a screen with carved scenes, which rose almost to
the level of the bases of the capitals. The altar was low, and
of stone, and possessed a re-table on which was placed a
cross. Enclosing it on all sides, save that towards the church,
was a screen with hangings of tapestry. At the four corners
of this screen were tall figures of angels. Immediately behind
the altar, and towering over it, was the shrine of St. Marcel, a
lofty open structure of brass and other metals in two stages,
ending in a gable at the apex of which rose a crucifix.
     On the first stage, so that it could be seen from all parts
of the choir, was the feretrum or reliquary of St. Marcel.
This chief shrine had on its side shrines of less importance,
while, in the background to the north, was the small altar of
the Trinity, on which was placed the reliquary of Notre Dame,
containing portions of the dress and other relics of the mother
of Christ. A few fine tombs were also in the sanctuary, and

G

not far away was a bronze statue of Eudes de Sully.   An
illustration, partly conjectural, of the choir and sanctuary in
the condition which I have attempted to describe from
Viollet-le-Duc's *Dictionnaire*, is reproduced here.   It will be
seen that while the furniture and ornament of this part of
the church is sufficiently splendid, it is nevertheless simple.
There would be ample space for the due performance of the

Photo]   [*Ed. Hautecœur, Paris. -*
GRILLE AT ENTRANCE OF CHOIR.

great ceremonials which constantly took place.   Such was the
appearance of the choir and sanctuary until Louis XIV., in
fulfilment of the vow of Louis XIII., who had dedicated
himself and his kingdom to the Virgin, began his transfor-
mation.
· The **Choir** is raised above the body of the church by three
steps, and on the right and left hand is enclosed by a low
grille in wrought iron with gilding.   This rests on a stone
foundation, and is terminated towards the centre by two

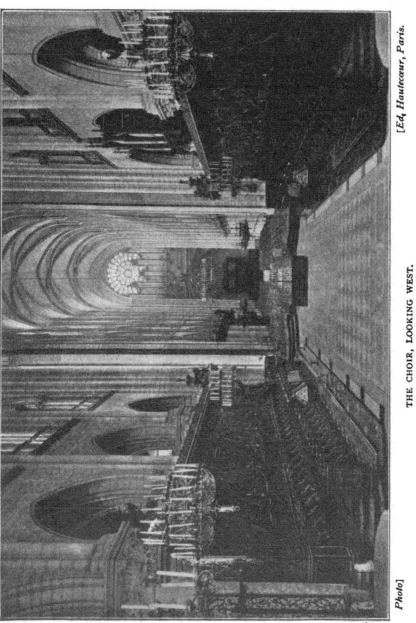

Photo]

THE CHOIR, LOOKING WEST.

[*Ed, Hautecœur, Paris.*]

massive columns, on which are hung the gates, which are of very beautiful design, representing conventionalised foliage and flowers.   At the top of the gate, in the centre, is a foliated cross.   The two bays on the south side of the choir nearest the entrance have the same arrangement of a small pointed window with a rose window beneath it, as exists in the side of the transept immediately adjacent.   The remaining windows are in the altered and enlarged form, and the triforium of the choir is similar to, though of earlier date than, that which runs round the nave.

The **Stalls** occupy three bays on either side of the choir. The erection of these stalls is part of the work undertaken by order of Louis XIV. in accomplishment of his father's vow, and it follows that they are not in character with the architecture of the choir.   It was once proposed that for this reason new stalls of " Gothic " design should take their place. There is little likelihood of this being done now.   Incongruity among things beautiful in themselves is by no means a calamity, and we may fairly question alike the taste and the learning of those who crave for uniformity at all cost.   One is glad to think that Viollet-le-Duc never for a moment contemplated the banishment of these stalls, which are a particularly fine example of the best work of which the craftsmen of the time were capable.   The stalls have been rearranged since they were first placed in the choir, and their number has diminished.   Originally there were one hundred and fourteen stalls ; now there are ten less.   They are divided on each side into upper and lower tiers, each tier having twenty-six seats.   The carvings are the work of Jean Nel and Louis Marteau, the designs being supplied by Jean de Goulon.   The designer and the executants have combined to produce a really admirable piece of work, of which a full account is given in a very careful monograph, published by Chouvet in Paris in 1855, entitled *Album des Boiseries sculptées du Chœur de Notre Dame de Paris.*   In this volume the carvings are dealt with one by one, and their merits intelligently discussed.   At the back of the upper row of stalls are eight large carved panels, which represent scenes in the life of the Virgin.   At the west end of the stalls are placed, opposite to one another, the throne of the archbishop and a similar throne for the dean of the chapter.   These thrones or seats have elaborately-carved canopies. The relief on the back of the chair or throne on the right represents the cure of Childebert I. by St. Germain, Bishop of Paris. On the opposite chair is represented in similar style the martyrdom of St. Denis. Throughout the entire cathedral, in sculpture, in stained glass, in carving, the Virgin is glorified, and next to her in honour comes St. Denis. The stalls are lighted by lamps in metal brackets, and the choir itself is illuminated by handsome candelabra similar to those in the nave. In the second bay on the north side of the choir is a small organ used in the daily offices.

Close by this organ the stones of the pavement are movable, and cover the entrance of a small crypt. This is the principal subterranean chamber of the cathedral, and it was constructed so recently as the eighteenth century. It was set apart as the burial place of the Archbishops of Paris, and is little more than a vault. Over the coffins of those of the Archbishops who have been Cardinals are suspended their red hats and tassels. The excavations for this little crypt led to a discovery which was of great interest to archæologists. Amongst other Roman remains was a small altar to Jupiter, which is now preserved in the Cluny Museum. In *Paris à travers les Ages* we read of a small crypt below the Chapelle S. Anne, on the south side of the nave. Used now as a coal cellar, it was formerly a burial place, as is attested by the following inscription : " Cave pour les cercueils de plomb ; cave pour la sépulture des chanoines ; caves pour la sépulture des musiciens, enfants de Chœurs et officiers clercs."

The pavement of the choir is of pieces of marble of various colours, which together form a geometrical pattern. As one looks at it, one laments the magnificent tombs with bronze effigies which were formerly the glory of this part of the church.

The **Sanctuary** is approached by four steps of Languedoc marble, and three additional steps of the same material lead to the high altar. The **High Altar** still retains most of the leading features of the arrangement of Louis XIV. It was begun in 1699, and finished in 1714. The pseudo-classical architecture by means of which the great pillars of the apse were hidden has of course been swept away. The principal group of sculpture, representing the Descent from the

THE CHOIR FROM THE SOUTH TRANSEPT.

Cross, is by Nicolas Coustou, who was born at Lyons in 1658. He was a pupil of Coysevox, his uncle, who at that time was director of the Academy of Painting and Sculpture at Paris. He obtained the *grand prix*, and went to study at Rome, where he was profoundly influenced by the work of Michael Angelo. Coustou's output on his return to France was enormous. The " Descent from the Cross," at Notre Dame was doubtless inspired by the famous group by Michael Angelo in St. Peter's at Rome.   It cannot be said that Coustou has approached the greatest of the Italians in the profundity of his pathos or in tragic solemnity, but the group at Notre Dame is not without decided merit, although it leans towards the melodramatic and artificial.

On one side of the altar is a kneeling statue of Louis XIII. by Guillaume Coustou, and on the other a similar statue of Louis XIV. by Antoine Coyevox. Guillaume Coustou was the younger brother of Nicolas, and like him studied at Rome. He represents Louis XIII. offering his crown and sceptre, which he holds in his hands, to the Virgin. The statue of Louis XIV. suggests the accomplishment of his father's vow. Coysevox, from whose chisel it came, was the leading French sculptor of his time. He was born at Lyons in 1640, and died in 1720. The statues of angels bearing the instruments of the Passion are by various sculptors. The angel with the crown of thorns and that carrying the reed are by Corneille Van Clève. The angel with the nails is by Claude Poirier ; that with the sponge by Simon Hurtrelle ; that with the scroll by Laurent Magnier ; and that with the lance by Anselme Flamen. The bas-relief in bronze-gilt in front of the altar represents the Entombment, and is by Van Clève. The cross and candelabra formerly belonged to the cathedral of Arras. The lectern of sculptured bronze is dated 1755, and has on its base the name of Duplessis, founder to the King. A superb example of Gobelins tapestry, the gift of Napoleon I., is used on great festivals to cover the floor of the sanctuary. The pavement is partly in mosaic, and has a representation of the arms of France.

The comparatively new stained glass of the choir and apse is not so bad as one might expect. It is by Maréchal of Metz. The central window of the apse is devoted to the Visitation. To the right are Eudes de Sully and St. Marcel ;

St. Augustine and St. Jerome; St. Luke and St. John; Daniel and Jeremiah; David and Abraham; St. George and St. Martin; Charlemagne and Pope Leo. III.; and St. Hilaire and St. Irénée. To the right the subjects are St. Denis and Maurice de Sully; St. Gregory and St. Ambrose; St. Mark and St. Matthew; Ezekiel and Isaiah; Aaron and Melchisedec; St. Stephen and St. Laurent, St. Louis and St. Gregory VII., and St. Remi and St. Martin. The small rose windows of the choir, like those of the transept, are filled with glass by Steinheil. The choir, more perhaps than any other part of the cathedral, has suffered from the wholesale destruction of glass which has already been described. Visitors to the cathedral of Chartres can estimate the value of mediæval glass in a Gothic cathedral. It is unfortunate that the great windows of the clerestory at Paris were filled up before the notable revival in the art of stained glass, which commenced in England, and has now extended to France.

We must now return to the Ambulatory and the adjacent chapels. It is in this part of the church that Viollet-le-Duc's decorations are most profuse, and it is not possible to consider them successful. It is quite probable that no such scheme of decoration could be open to fewer objections than that of Viollet-le-Duc. The truth is that the colour confuses our appreciation of the fine lines of the architecture, and it is frequently restless and irritating where it should be most reposeful.

The Chapels of the Choir. On the south side are the following chapels :—

Chapelle Saint-Denis. The chief object of interest here is a statue, by Auguste de Bay, of Archbishop Affre, who is represented at the moment when he made his heroic appearance on the barricade of the Faubourg Saint Antoine with an olive branch. This was on June 25th, 1848, during the Commune. The Archbishop was struck by a ball and killed.

Chapelle Sainte-Madeleine. This chapel contains the grave of the Papal nuncio Garibaldi, Archbishop of Myra, who died in 1853. Archbishop Sibor, who was murdered in the church of St. Etienne du Mont on Jan. 8th, 1857, by a priest, is commemorated by a kneeling statue in marble by Dubois.

Chapelle Saint-Guillaume. The statue of the Virgin seated, with the Child Jesus in her arms, is attributed to Bernini, who came from Rome to Paris during the reign of Louis XIV. to make alterations and additions to the Louvre.   The Mausoleum of Henri-Charles d'Harcourt, Lieutenant-general of the armies of the King, who died in 1769, is a pretentious and theatrical work which was once highly esteemed.   It is by the sculptor Pigalle, and is of white marble.   The widow who kneels by the tomb and appears to be calling her husband is warned away by a figure of Death.   The genius of War is represented lamenting, and the whole is completed by trophies of arms.

Chapelle Saint-Georges.   Amongst the elaborate mural decorations of this chapel is a picture by Steinheil of St. George and the Dragon.   The statue of Archbishop Darboy is by Bonnassieux.   The prelate is represented falling amidst the bullets of the Communists, whom he blesses as he dies.   This tragic incident took place in the prison of La Roquette, on May 27th, 1871.   Close by is a kneeling statue of Archbishop Morlot (*d.* 1862) by Lescorné.   The chapel also contains a statue of St. George by the same artist.

The following are the chapels on the *north* side of the choir :—

La Chapelle de Notre Dame des Sept Douleurs, or *La Chapelle du Petit Chœur.*   The bas-reliefs over the altar represent the angel appearing to the Virgin Mary, the Descent from the Cross, and the Entombment.   The statue in wood of Notre Dame des Sept Douleurs is by Corbon.   The compositions, in six panels, by Perrodin, represent : Jesus bearing the Cross ; Christ on Calvary ; the Descent from the Cross ; the Communion of the Virgin ; and the Death of the Virgin.   The nine carved wood stalls are of the same period as those of the choir.   They were possibly part of the original series, which, as we have seen, was reduced in number.   At all events, the details indicate that the same designer and craftsmen were employed on them.   This chapel contains the only important fragment of the original polychromatic decoration with which the walls of the cathedral were anciently embellished. It consists of a mural painting dating from the fourteenth century.   In the centre is represented the Virgin enthroned with the Child.   To the right is St. Denis, and on the left Bishop Simon Matiffas de Buci, who built the three chapels on the left of the apse.   Beneath the picture was formerly the

Bishop's tomb. Below the representation of the Virgin and Child is a curious design representing angels bearing away a human soul. This painting was unfortunately restored by M. Maillot the elder, and has consequently lost much of its antiquarian interest.

Chapelle Saint-Marcel. Pierre Deseine's enormous monument to Cardinal de Belloy fills a large part of this chapel. The cardinal is represented giving alms to two orphan girls. St. Denis looks on, and records the cardinal's name on a list of the bishops of Paris noted for their charity. Close by is the tomb, with reclining figure, of Monseigneur de Quelen, by De Chaume. Amongst the mural decorations of this chapel the chief is a large painting by Maillot the younger. The subject is the "Translation of the relics of St. Marcel from the old Church of St. Marie to the Church of Notre Dame by Bishop Eudes de Sully." The personages represented are portraits of the officials of the diocese, and include Archbishop Darboy and the Abbé la Place. In the vaulting is a design representing the Coronation of St. Marcel.

Chapelle Saint-Louis. This chapel has six statues in wood by Corbon, representing Christ, the Virgin, St. John, St. Denis, St. Rustiguex, and St. Eleutherius. The kneeling statue of Archbishop Louis-Antoine de Noailles, who died in 1729, is by De Chaume.

Chapelle Saint-Germain. Tomb of Archbishop Leclercq de Juigné (died 1811), a kneeling figure in relief. The tomb was repaired by Viollet-le-Duc, who modified its original design.

Chapelle Saint-Ferdinand. Monument of Archbishop de Beaumont (died 1781), from designs by Viollet-le-Duc.

Chapelle Saint-Martin. Monument of Jean-Baptiste de Vardes, Comte de Guébriant, Marshal of France, who died in 1643, and of his wife Renée du Bec Crespin. A splendid service was celebrated in Notre Dame on the Marshal's death. His wife was sent to Poland as ambassadress extraordinary, and died there in 1643, without being able to erect a monument to her husband. The Marquis de Vardes erected the tomb, which was practically destroyed during the Revolution. It was renewed from designs by Viollet-le-Duc.

Behind the Sanctuary is the tomb with a jewelled effigy of Archbishop Matiffas de Buci, who died in 1304. It was removed from La Chapelle de Notre Dame des Sept Douleurs. In the arcading below the bas-reliefs of Jehan Revy and Jean le Bouteiller are placed little brasses with the names, arms, and date of the death of the persons whose remains are buried at Notre Dame. A list of the most interesting of these has already been given.

THE PLACE DU PARVIS IN 1650.
(From an engraving by Van Merlen.)

CHAPTER VI.

CONCLUSION.   THE SACRISTY, ETC.

NOTRE DAME was within comparatively recent times surrounded with streets so narrow that vehicular traffic was
impossible.   Amongst the most characteristic were the Rue
de Glatigny and the Rue de Marmousets, which, as late as
1865, preserved the dimensions, and something of the aspect,
of a side street in the middle ages.   The *quartier* thus
intersected literally teemed with churches of which nothing
remains.   Amongst them perhaps the most important were
those dedicated to Saint-Landry, Sainte-Geneviève des Ardents,
Saint-Pierre aux Bœufs, Saint-Aguan, Saint-Marine, Saint-Luc,
Saint-Jean le Rond, Saint-Denis au Pays and Saint-Christophe.
None of them appear to have been large, and of some the
origin and history remain obscure.

On the south side of the Cathedral stood the *Palais
Episcopal*, which was constructed by Maurice de Sully and
added to by Matiffas de Bucy and other prelates.   On
Feb. 14th, 1831, it was attacked by the mob, and five
hours sufficed for its complete destruction.   The contents
included a library of 20,000 volumes, a collection of 1,500

manuscripts, those of the ancient archives of the church, which escaped the Revolutionists, a fine collection of pictures, and priceless works of art of an ecclesiastical character. These were thrown into the Seine, burned, or stolen.

The **Cloîture** or Cloister of Notre Dame was on the north side and at the east end of the church. It is difficult to say what was its early aspect, but in the sixteenth century and afterwards it in no way resembled the cloister of a monastery, but consisted of an agglomeration of separate houses. It was in the nature of a College of Secular Canons. It was similar to the Temple in London in that it possessed gates of its own, which shut it off from the rest of the city. The Cloister contained thirty-seven houses for the canons of the Cathedral, who were allowed to have living with them their near female relatives. No other women, lay or religious, were allowed to sleep in the cloister. The tedious Rue du Cloître Notre-Dame occupies a portion of the space on which the Cloister stood.

The **Sacristy** was formerly a part of the Palais Episcopal. It had been rebuilt by Soufflot, whose work was partially destroyed in 1831. A new sacristy has been constructed by Viollet-le-Duc in the style of the thirteenth century. The exterior is richly ornamented with statues and pinnacles. It communicates with the south ambulatory of the choir by means of two covered passages, one of which leads into the *Sacristie du Chapitre*, which contains a large hall, the room of the Chapter above, which is the cathedral treasury, and a vestry for the canons. The great hall has stained glass windows in which bishops of Paris are represented.

It contains a crucifix and two statuettes by Corbon, a fine *armoire* decorated with paintings of scenes in the life of St. Denis. There are pictures in various parts of the building by Vaulos, Salvator Rosa, Lebrun, Louis Testelin, Charles Poerson and others, but none of them are of much note. A picturesque little cloister, with a fountain in the middle surmounted by a crucifix, is one of the agreeable features of the building. Its eastern arcade is glazed, the windows representing scenes in the life of Ste. Geneviève.

The **Treasury**, once endowed with enormous riches, was despoiled at the Revolution of all but a few objects of value. There still remains the reputed Crown of Thorns (supposed to have been given to St. Louis), brought hither from La Sainte Chapelle. The so-called Nail of the True Cross formerly belonged to the royal abbey of St. Denis. These relics are only exposed on Fridays in Lent. The reliquaries are for the most part imitations of those which were formerly in La Sainte Chapelle. Perhaps the most interesting of the objects exhibited is a gold cross, probably of twelfth-century workmanship. It belonged to the Emperor Manuel Comnenus, and was bequeathed by the Princess Anne de Gonzague to the church of St. Germain des Près in 1863. In addition there are the relic of the True Cross sent to Bishop Galon in 1109, from the Church of the Holy Sepulchre in Jerusalem ; the " discipline" of St. Louis ; the crozier in copper and wood of Bishop Eudes de Sully ; the crucifix used by St. Vincent-de-Paul at the death-bed of Louis XIII. ; the pastoral cross of Archbishop Affre ; a silver image of the Virgin and Child presented in 1821 by Charles X. ; the *ostensoir* given by Napoleon I., and services of plate presented by the same monarch and by Napoleon III. The vestments are very magnificent, and include the coronation mantle of Napoleon I. and the chasuble worn by Pope Pius VI. when he crowned him. The *soutanes* worn by Archbishops Affre, Sibour, and Darboy in their last moments, marked by the instruments which pro-duced their violent deaths, have a tragic interest.

The somewhat obtrusively picturesque modern building to the west of the Sacristy is known as the *Presbytère*. It has been often ridiculed, and at times rather fiercely denounced, but if any building was to be erected on the site, it seems difficult to imagine anything less offensive. It is pleasing and unpretentious, and contrasts only too favourably with the dull houses of the Rue du Cloîture Notre-Dame, which are as undistinguished as they well can be.

The space at the back of the Cathedral is laid out as a garden. This is modern and somewhat formal, but it affords a fine view of the east end, and constitutes a welcome oasis of trees and grass in a grey waste of commonplace buildings. In the centre is a fountain with a statue of the Virgin and Child, and fragments of sculpture and carving taken from the church at different times lie about. The reader who wishes to under-stand at a glance the various changes which have taken place in that part of the French metropolis which lies in the very shadow of the cathedral should refer to the second volume of the magnificent work *Paris à travers les Ages*, in which a plan of the district in 1881 is compared with conjectural plans of the same in the years 1150, 1550, and 1750.

The huge open space west of the cathedral is the Place du Parvis Notre-Dame. This oblong *place* far exceeds the church itself in area, and gives to the west front a somewhat dwarfed appearance. On the left-hand side (looking east) is the vast Hotel Dieu, the modern name of the hospital, known as the Maison Dieu, which for centuries has been associated with Notre Dame. The present building was only completed in 1877. It is from the designs of M. Diet, and is by no means of an ornamental character, although the total cost was 36,400,000 francs. On the west side of the Place du Parvis are the barracks of the Garde Republicaine. Close to them is one of those open-air flower markets which are so charming and characteristic a feature of the Paris of to-day.

H

NOTRE DAME IN THE XIII CENTURY, SHOWING THE BISHOP'S PALACE
(L'ÉVÊCHÉ) ON THE LEFT.

(From " Paris à travers les Ages.")

CHAPTER VII.

LIST OF THE BISHOPS AND ARCHBISHOPS OF PARIS.

(I have adopted the spelling and dates generally given by French Catholic writers in compiling this list).

ST. DENIS, who is counted as the first bishop by Roman Catholic writers, is said to have been succeeded by the following, of whom little or nothing is known: Mallo or Mallon; Massus; Marcus; Adventus; Ventorien; Paul; Prudence; St. Marcel (died about 436); Vivien; Felix; Flavien; Ursicien; Apedemius; Heraclitus (? 490–525); Probat; Amelius;

Saffarac (545–552).
Eusèbe I. (552–555).
St. Germain (555–576).
Raguemond (576–591).
Eusèbe II. (592–594).

Faramode (?); Simplicius (?); Saint Céran (606–621); Leudebert (?); Aubert.

St. Landry (650–656).

Chrodobert (656–663).

Sigobrand (663–664).

Importun (?).

St. Agilbert (666–680).

Sigefroid (?); Tournsaede (?); Adolphe (?); Bernechaire, (?).

St. Hugues (722–730).

Marséide.

Fédole (?); Raguecapt (?); Madalbert (?); Desdefroid (?); Escheurade (?).

Ermenfroi (?)

Inchalde (809–831).

Ercheurade (831–857).

Enée (857–883).

Ingelvin (?).

Gozlin (883–886).

Anschéric (886–911).

Théodulphe or Gendulphe (911–922). This bishop is believed to have been succeeded by Falrade; Adelhelme; Gauthier I.; Albéric; Constante; Garin; Rainaud I.; Elisiard, and Giselbert.

Renault II., de Vendome (992–1019).

Azelin or Albert (?).

Francon (1020–1030).

Imbert Hesselin (1030–1060).

Godefroi de Boulogne (1061–1093).

Guillaume I. de Montfort (1095–1102).

Foulques I (1102–1104).

Galon (1105–1116).

Giselbert or Gilbert (1116–1124).

Etienne I. de Senlis (1124–1142).

Thiébault (1143–1157).

Pierre Lombard (1158–1159).

Maurice de Sully (1160–1196).

Eudes de Sully (1197–1208).

Pierre II. de Nemours (1208–1219).

Guillaume de Seiguelay (1220–1223)

Barthélemy (1223–1227).

(The see is believed to have been vacant for a year)

Guillaume d'Auvergne (also called Guillaume de Paris) (1228–1249).

Gauthier II. de Chateau-Thierry (1249–1250).
Renault III. de Corbeil (1250–1268).
Etienne II. (1268–1279).
Ranulfe ou Raoul d'Homblières (1279–1288).
Simon Matiffas de Bucy (1290–1304).
Guillaume IV. de Baufet (1304–1319).
Etienne de Bourret (1320–1325).
Hugues II. (1326–1332).
Guillaume V. de Chanac (1332–1342).
Foulques II. (1342–1349).
Audoin Aubert (?).
Pierre III. de la Forêt (1350–1352).
Jean I. de Meulan (1352–1363).
Etienne IV. de Paris (1363–1368).
Aimeric de Maignac (1368–1384).
Pierre IV. d'Orgement (1384–1409.
Gérard de Montaigu (1409–1420).
Jean II. de Courte-Cuisse (1421–1422).
Jean III. de la Roche-Taillé (1422–1423).
Jean IV. de Nant (1423–1427).
Jacques de Chastelier (1427–1439).
Denis II. du Moulin (1439–1447).
Guillaume VI. Chartier (1447–1472).
Louis de Beaumont (1473–1492).
Gerard Goballie (1494).
Jean V., Simon de Champigny (1494–1502).
Etienne V., Poncher (1503–1519).
François de Poncher (1519–1532).
Jean VI. de Bellay (1532–1551).
Eustache de Bellay (1551–1564).
Guillaume Viole (1564–1568).
Cardinal Pierre V. de Gondi (1568–1598).
Cardinal Henri de Gondi de Retz (1598–1622).

ARCHBISHOPS.

Paris was raised to the rank of an archbishopric on the demand of Louis XIII. to Pope Gregory XV. (The Bull is dated Oct. 20th, 1622.)

1. Jean-François de Gondi (1622–1654). First Archbishop of Paris. Buried in Notre Dame.

2. Jean-François-Paul de Gondi (Cardinal de Retz). Buried in Saint-Denis (1654–1679).

3. Pierre VI. de Marca (*d.* 1662). Buried in Notre Dame.

4. Hardouin de Péréfix de Beaumont (*d.* 1671). Buried in Notre Dame.

5. François de Harlay de Champvallon (*d.* 1695). Buried in Notre Dame.

6. Louis-Antoine de Noailles. Cardinal (*d.* 1729). Buried in Notre Dame.

7. Charles-Gaspard-Guillaume de Vintimille du Luc (*d.* 1746). Buried in Notre Dame.

8. Jacques-Bonnet-Gigault de Bellefonds (*d.* 1746). Buried in Notre Dame.

9. Christophe de Beaumont du Repaire (*d.* 1781). Buried in Notre Dame.

10. Antoine-Eléonore-Léon Le Clerc de Juigné de Neuchelle (*d.* 1811). Buried in Notre Dame.

11. Jean-Baptiste de Belloy. Cardinal. Died, aged ninety-eight years and eight months, in 1808, and buried in Notre Dame.

12. Alexandre-Angélique de Tallyrand-Perigord. Born 1736. Archbishop of Reims 1776. Cardinal 1817 ; Died 1821.

13. Hyacinthe-Louis de Quélen. Born 1778. Bishop of Samosate 1817 ; Archbishop of Paris 1821. Died 1839.

14. Denis III., Auguste Affre. Born 1793. Archbishop of Paris 1840. Struck by a ball at the barricades in the Faubourg Saint-Antoine on June 25th, 1848, and died two days later.

15. Marie-Dominique-Auguste Sibour. Born 1792. Bishop of Digue 1839 ; Archbishop of Paris 1848. Was assassinated on Jan. 3rd, 1857, in the church of Saint-Etienne du Mont by a priest. He had as auxiliary bishop Léon-François Sibour.

16. François III., Nicolas-Madeleine Morlot. Born 1795. Bishop of Orléans 1839 ; Archbishop of Tours 1842 ; Cardinal 1853 ; Archbishop of Paris 1857. Died 1862.

17. Georges Darboy. Born 1813. Bishop of Nancy 1850 ; Archbishop of Paris 1863. Arrested as a hostage by the Commune on April 4th, 1871, and shot on May 27th.

18. Joseph-Hippolyte Guibert. Born 1802. Archbishop of Tours 1857 ; Archbishop of Paris 1871 ; Cardinal 1873. Died 1886.

19. François-Marie-Benjamin Richard. Born 1819. Bishop of Belley 1871 ; Coadjutor of Archbishop Guibert 1875 ; Archbishop of Paris 1886. Cardinal 1889.

INDEX

CHISWICK PRESS: PRINTED BY CHARLES WHITTINGHAM AND CO.
TOOKS COURT, CHANCERY LANE, LONDON.

INTERNAL DIMENSIONS.

Length (total)	. . . .	390	feet.
,, of nave	. . . .	225	,,
,, of transepts	. . . . . .	144	,,
Width of nave vault	. . . . . .	39	,,
Height of ,, ,,	. . . . . .	102	,,
,, ,, towers .	. . . . .	204	,,
Area . . .	. . . . .	54,050	sq. feet.

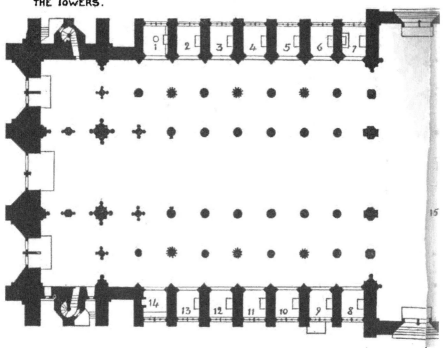

ENTRANCE TO
THE TOWERS.

SCALE OF FEET.

1. Chapelle des Fonts Baptismaux.
2. Chapelle Saint-Charles.
3.   „   de la Sainte-Enfance.
4.   „   Saint - Vincent - de -
Paul.
5. Chapelle de Saint - François-
Xavier.
6. Chapelle de Saint-Landry.
7.   „   de Sainte-Clotilde.
8. Chapelle de l'Annonciation.
9.   „   du Sacré Cœur.
10.   „   Sainte-Anne.
11.   „   Saint-Pierre.
12.   „   Saint-Joseph.
13.   „   Sainte-Geneviève.
14.   „   des Ames du Purgatoire.
15. Statue of Notre Dame de
Paris.

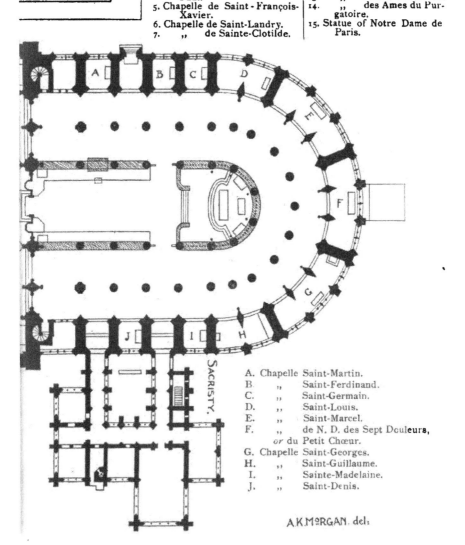

A. Chapelle Saint-Martin.
B.   „   Saint-Ferdinand.
C.   „   Saint-Germain.
D.   „   Saint-Louis.
E.   „   Saint-Marcel.
F.   „   de N. D. des Sept Douleurs,
    or du Petit Chœur.
G. Chapelle Saint-Georges.
H.   „   Saint-Guillaume.
I.   „   Sainte-Madelaine.
J.   „   Saint-Denis.

A.K.MᶜRGAN del.

CPSIA information can be obtained
at www.ICGtesting.com
Printed in the USA
BVHW042141150419
545617BV00006B/28/P